Photoshop 6.0

Christopher Lumgair

TEACH YOURSELF BOOKS

Trademarks

Many of the designations used by manufacturers and sellers to distinguish their products are claimed as trademarks. Where those designations appear in this book, and Hodder & Stoughton was aware of the trademark claim, the designations have been printed in initial caps or all caps.

For UK orders queries: please contact Bookpoint Ltd, 130 Milton Park, Abingdon, Oxon OX14 4SB. Telephone: (44) 01235 827720. Fax: (44) 01235 400454. Lines are open from 9.00–18.00, Monday to Saturday, with a 24-hour message answering service. Email address: orders@bookpoint.co.uk.

For U.S.A order queries: please contact McGraw-Hill Customer Services, P.O. Box 545, Blacklick, OH 43004-0545, U.S.A. Telephone: 1-800-722-4726. Fax: 1-614-755-5645.

For Canada order queries: please contact McGraw-Hill Ryerson Ltd, 300 Water Street, Whitby, Ontario L1N 9B6, Canada. Telephone: 905 430 5000, Fax: 905 430 5020.

Long renowned as the authoritative source of self-guided learning – with more than 30 million copies sold worldwide – the *Teach Yourself* series includes over 300 titles in the fields of languages, crafts, hobbies, business and education.

British Library Cataloguing in Publication Data
A catalogue record for this title is available from The British Library.

Library of Congress Catalog Card Number: On file

First published in UK 2001 by Hodder Headline Plc, 338 Euston Road, London NW1 3BH.

First published in US 2001 by Contemporary Books, A Division of The MacGraw-Hill Companies, 1 Prudential Plaza, 130 East Randolph Street, Chicago, Illinois 60601 U.S.A.

Printed in Great Britain for Hodder & Stoughton Educational, a division of Hodder Headline Plc, 338 Euston Road, London NW1 3BH by Cox & Wyman Ltd, Reading, Berkshire.

Impression number 10 9 8 7 6 5 4 3 2
Year 2007 2006 2005 2004 2003 2002

CONTENTS

1 INTRODUCTION

This book has a simple purpose: to introduce complete beginners to digital image processing using Adobe Photoshop 6.0 and teach the necessary skills they will need to enhance, retouch and compose still images.

In aiming to give readers a good grounding in the use of the program, I have concentrated on those controls, techniques and processes essential to the creation of sound, well-balanced imagery, whatever the subject matter or final use.

Multimedia in all its manifestations has meant that the computer has become a medium in its own right rather than just a tool. Digital images are now as likely to be integrated into web pages and multimedia projects as into DTP documents and I have kept this in mind throughout the book.

To this end I have devoted a chapter to ImageReady, the web program that's bundled with Photoshop 6.0. I show you how to create web pages from image composites, complete with roll-over buttons, image-maps and animations.

Whilst the version discussed is Photoshop 6.0, many of the core procedures can be achieved within versions 4.0 onwards.

Whether you are new to visual communications or already work in the graphic arts field, I hope you will find the book a useful guide to a remarkable image-processing tool.

Please e-mail me at pst@campbell-lumgair.com if you have any comments.

Overview of Photoshop

What is Photoshop?

Photoshop is an digital image-editing program, providing the user with a single environment in which image enhancement, retouching and the creation of image composites can be accomplished.

It includes:

- resizing and mode controls
- selection and masking facilities
- painting and editing tools
- pasting and layer controls
- tonal and colour correction controls
- vector tools
- special-effect filters
- slicing and optimizing controls
- image map, rollover and animation controls
- powerful colour conversion capabilities.

Bitmap images

Photoshop manipulates and processes bitmap images created using scanning or photographic methods. A bitmap image can be described as a mosaic of picture elements, each element representing a single tone or colour.

Mode and resolution

Whether elements within an image are just black or white or one of a range of tones or colours is determined by its mode. The density of picture elements (the number of pixels per inch) is determined by its resolution. Image mode, resolution and dimensions are set at the image capture stage but are alterable at any time.

Paint effects

You can colour images using the painting tools in combination with the selection tools. These tools also enable you to originate and modify masks.

Retouching

You can retouch images using the editing tools in combination with selection and painting tools. These tools enable you to remove unwanted details within images or to improve on existing details.

Layers

You can cut and paste images within and between documents and create multi-layered image composites. You can rotate, flip, scale and distort images using the transformation commands.

Tones, colours and sharpness

You can improve the tones, colours, brightness and sharpness of an image by using the Adjust controls and sharpening filters.

Text, shapes and effects

You can add type to an image using the type tools and make simple graphic elements using the shape tools. Styles can be applied to type and shapes to create three-dimensional and other effects for rollover buttons and such like.

Web features

You can slice up image composites to create feature-rich web pages, complete with rollover buttons, image maps and animations. Furthermore you can optimize images, whether sliced or not, to achieve the right balance between download speed and image quality.

Outputting to print

You can convert colour images to the CMYK printing mode and save images in appropriate file formats for importing to DTP documents. You can output documents to desktop printers or imageset documents to produce bromides or colour separations.

Conventions used in this book

Keystrokes in the main text are shown as icons, such as [Control]

When icons are separated by a + sign, as in [⌘]+[+=], the modifier key(s) before the + sign should be held down (together) whilst the key after the + sign is pressed.

PC keyboards include an [Alt] instead of the [Option] key.

PC keyboards lack the Macintosh's [⌘] (Command) key. In all cases use the [Control] key instead.

Other icons in this book are used in the following contexts:

- ● Single-step instructions.
- ① Step-by-step instructions.
- ! Warnings and critical information.
- ▲ Helpful hints.
- ✚ Additional non-essential information.

Bitmap images are reproduced at varying resolutions throughout the book to communicate different points.

Vector items, such as anchor points and direction lines, are mainly illustrated as they appear on screen.

Dialog boxes and palettes are generally illustrated as they appear on a Macintosh.

Using this book

It's best to read this book in the order as written since some of the instructions assume knowledge gained in previous chapters. Having said this, feel free to dip into chapters as and when the need arises as the book's designed to also work as a ready-reference. You will undoubtedly need to refer to Chapter 1 every now and again whatever your approach, as it contains essential information about the selection and function of the tools.

2 THE PHOTOSHOP INTERFACE

This chapter is intended as a general reference to several features of the Photoshop interface, including the Photoshop document window, Options bar and palettes.

For those new to either the Macintosh or Windows, a sub-section covers the standard controls used within the program.

The controls on each platform work in a similar manner although their appearance is subject to differing visual standards (see Figure 2.1).

If you are familiar with either system you can skip this sub-section.

As far as the key Photoshop features are concerned, you may wish to just glance at the information and then move on, referring back to the section as and when necessary.

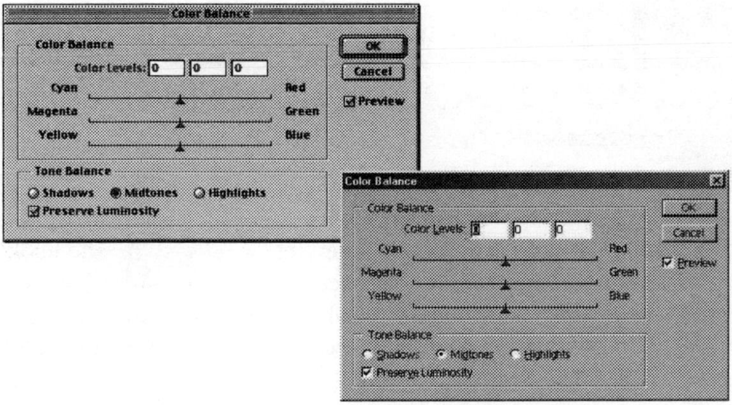

Figure 2.1 Windows control overlying the Macintosh equivalent

Document window and toolbox

The document window

The document window (Figure 2.2) displays an open Photoshop document.

Features include:

① title bar

② close box

③ zoom box

④ size box

⑤ image area

⑥ scroll bars

⑦ rulers

⑧ ruler origin

⑨ file sizes

⑩ mode

⑪ scale/scale field

⑫ page preview box.

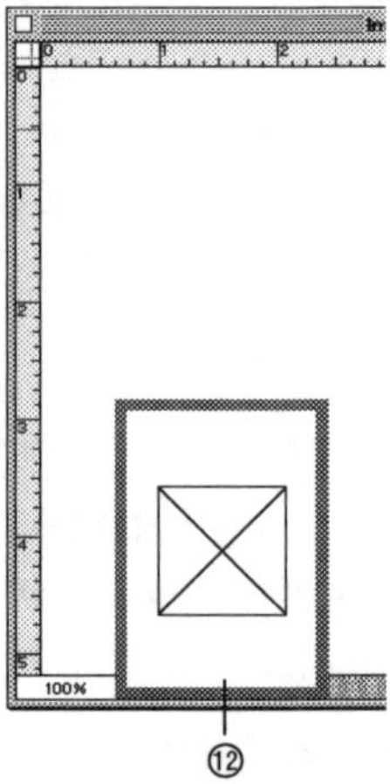

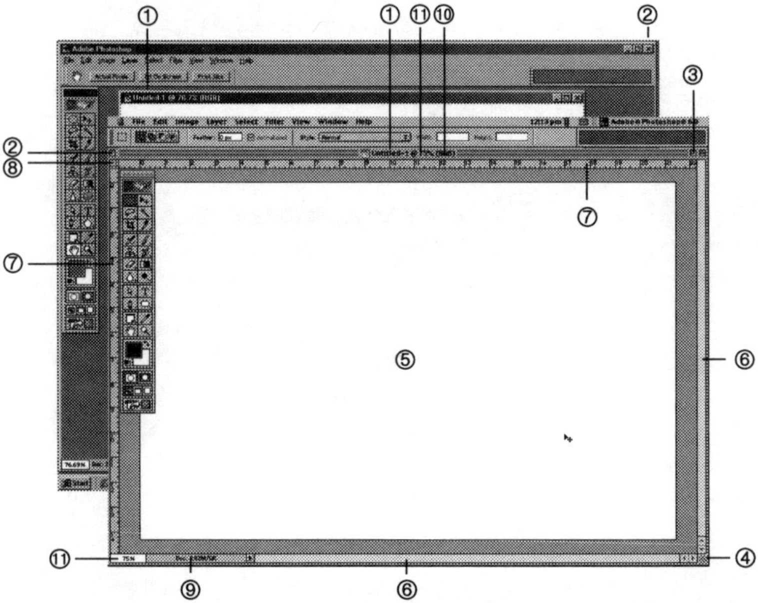

Figure 2.2 Macintosh document window overlaid over Windows version

The toolbox (Figure 2.3)

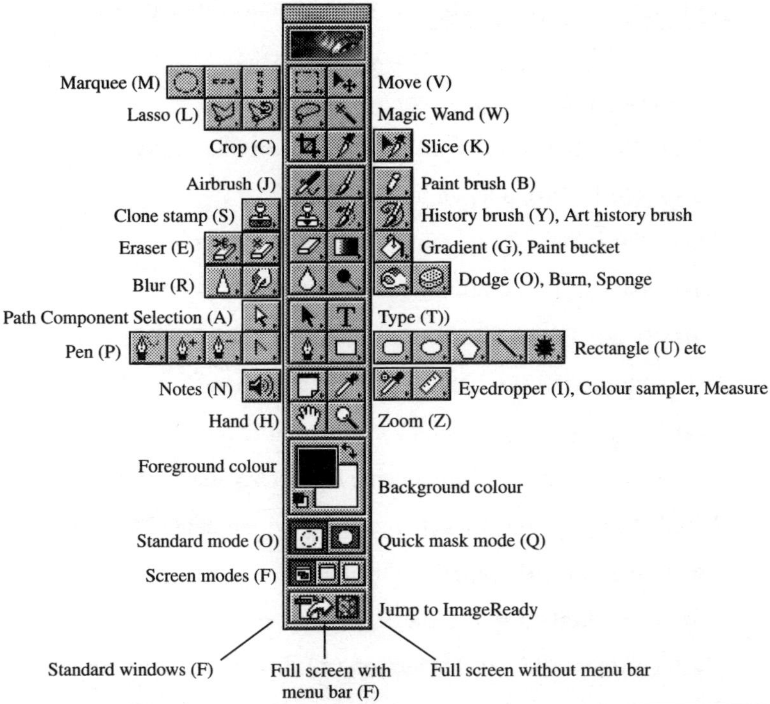

Figure 2.3 The toolbox

Selecting a tool

- Click once to select a tool. The pointer changes to the tool cursor. Click or click-drag on the image as appropriate.

▲ Press the Caps Lock key to turn icons into a cross-hair pointer for precision working.

Select tools sharing the same location within the palette by clicking or click-dragging to the tool in the 'pop-up' menu.

Press the Command (Control) key to temporarily access the Move tool (except when the Slice and Pen tools are selected).

Press the letters in parentheses for shortcuts to each tool.

Tools overview

Marquee (M): for selecting rectangular and elliptical areas

Move (V): for moving selections and layers

Lasso variants (L): for selecting shaped areas

Magic Wand (W): for selecting areas of similar colour

Crop (C): for cropping an image

Slice (K): for slicing up an image for web output

Airbrush (J): for painting with soft edges

Paint brush/Pencil (B): for painting with soft/hard edges

Clone stamp (S): for cloning parts of an image

History/Art history brush (Y): for painting back to a previous state

Eraser variants (E): for exposing the background colour

Gradient (G)/Paint bucket: for filling with gradated/flat colours

Focussing variants (R): for blurring and sharpening locally

Toning variants (O): for altering brightness/saturation locally

Path component/Direct selection (A): for selecting vector paths

Type (T): for entering and editing type

Pen variants (P): for drawing and editing vector paths

Shape variants (U): for drawing vector shapes and lines

Notes and audio annotation (N): for written and audio notes

Eyedropper (I): for selecting current colours

Hand (H): for scrolling the image within the document window

Zoom (Z): for altering the viewing scale

▲ Press the letters in parentheses for short-cuts to each tool.

Controlling the behaviour of tools

The behaviour of tools is controlled by settings in the Options bar (see Figure 2.4). This context-sensitive palette displays the correct options whatever tool is selected. It's permanently on view provided your screen resolution is greater than 800×600 pixels and it can be docked anywhere on the screen. If it's hidden for any reason, select any tool and it should reappear.

Options for the painting and editing tools include a pop-up Brushes panel for setting the size and shape of the tools and a palette well for storing palettes you wish to access at odd times.

Figure 2.4 The marquee tool options bar

Basic controls

Scroll bars

Every window within Photoshop has two scroll bars, one for vertical scrolling and one for horizontal scrolling. A grey scroll bar indicates more content beyond a window's borders; a clear bar indicates that all content is visible (see Figure 2.5).

Using the scroll bars

- Click the up, down, left or right scroll arrow.

  Or:

- Click the vertical or horizontal scroll bar on either side of the scroll box, when it's grey.

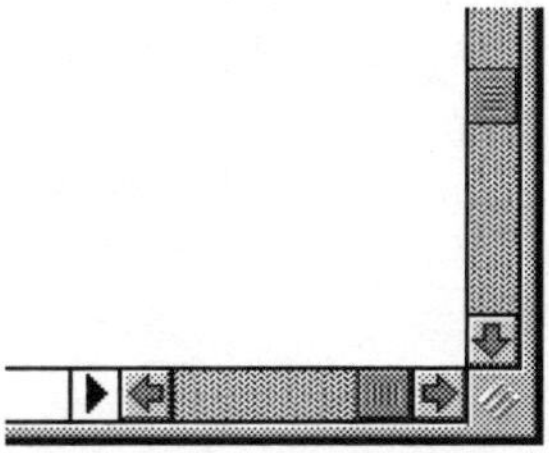

Figure 2.5 Vertical and horizontal scroll bars

Or:

- Drag the vertical or horizontal scroll box along its scroll bar.

Menus

Menus within Photoshop come in two types: pull-down menus and pop-up menus. The menus in the Photoshop menu bar are pull-down menus. Pop-up menus appear in palettes, dialog boxes or at the cursor, the latter being context-sensitive.

Selecting options from pull-down menus

- Point to the menu name, press to 'pull down' the menu, drag to the item you wish to choose so that it's highlighted and then release the mouse button.

Selecting options from pop-up menus

- Point to the visible menu item, press to 'pop up' the menu, drag to the item you wish to choose so that it's highlighted and then release the mouse button.

Selecting options from context-sensitive menus

- Hold down [Control], move the cursor over the object and press the mouse button. A menu appears (see Figure 2.6). Drag to the item you wish to choose so that it's highlighted and then release the mouse button.

▲ In Windows, there is no need to drag to the item you wish to choose in a menu. Just press on the menu name or item and the full menu will be displayed. Then click on the item you wish to choose.

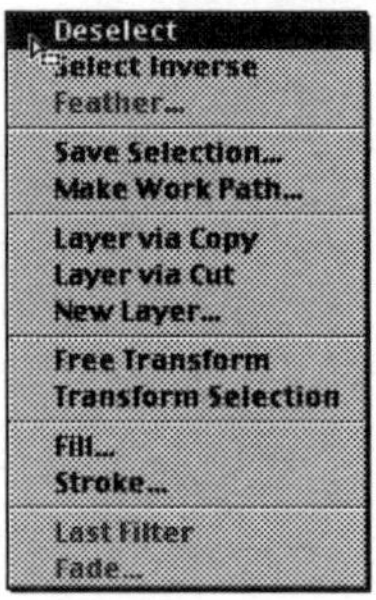

Figure 2.6 Example of a context-sensitive menu

Dialog boxes

In general, dialog boxes provide a means of specifying and applying artwork attributes. You can enter specifications into these boxes in a number of ways (see Figure 2.7). These boxes are modal so it's necessary to OK or cancel any settings before you can move on to other tasks.

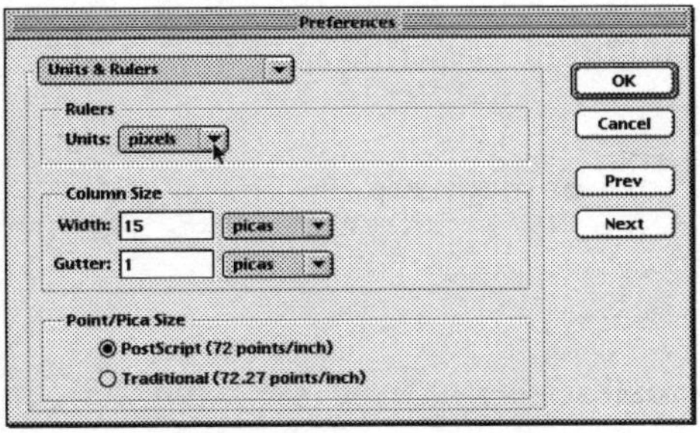

Figure 2.7 Dialog box with pop-up menus, fields and radio buttons

Entering new values in fields

① Double-click existing values (if not already highlighted).

② Type in new values.

Moving from field to field

- Press Tab

Checking boxes

Any number of boxes can be selected within a group of boxes.

- Click the box. An X or tick indicates that it's selected.

Clicking radio buttons

Only one button can be selected within a group of buttons.

- Click the button. An emboldened button indicates that it's selected.

Resetting specifications in dialog boxes

- Hold down Option to replace Cancel by Reset. Click Reset.

Applying specifications and closing box

- Click OK or press ↵ .

Palettes

Palettes provide a further means of specifying and applying drawing attributes. Although their sets of controls are similar to those found in dialog boxes (see Figure 2.7), they differ in that they can remain displayed at all times.

Furthermore, palettes in some cases can be extended (see Figure 2.8) to show further options. They can also be nested together to save screen space.

Bringing a palette to the front of its group

- Click the palette's tab.

Displaying palette

- Choose the palette from the Window menu (see Figure 2.8).

Entering new values in fields

Either:

① Double-click existing values (if not already highlighted).

② Type in new values.

③ Press Enter.

Or:

① Click either of the small triangles to increase or decrease a value.

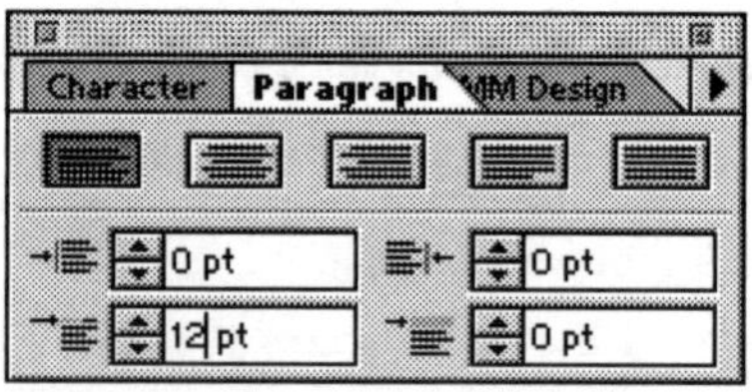

Figure 2.8 Entering a value by typing into a palette field

Moving from field to field

- Press Tab
- Choose Show Options from a palette's pop-menu (see Figure 2.9.

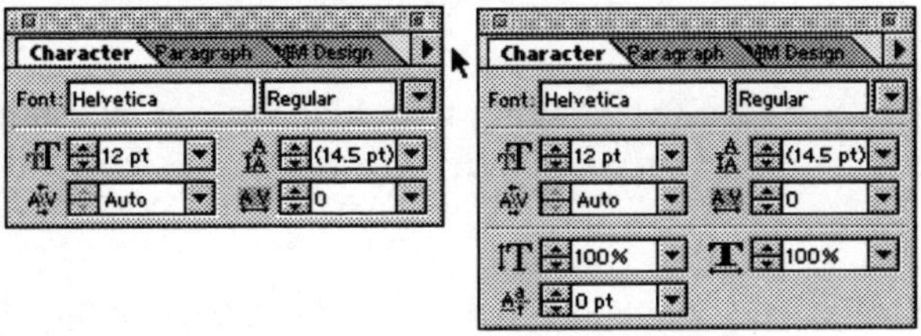

Figure 2.9 Example of palette in short and extended form

Nesting palettes

- Click-drag tab (named area) of palette to within area of palette in which you wish it to nest.

▲ You can nest palettes in the palette well, the dark grey panel at the right end of the Options bar (see Figure 2.10).

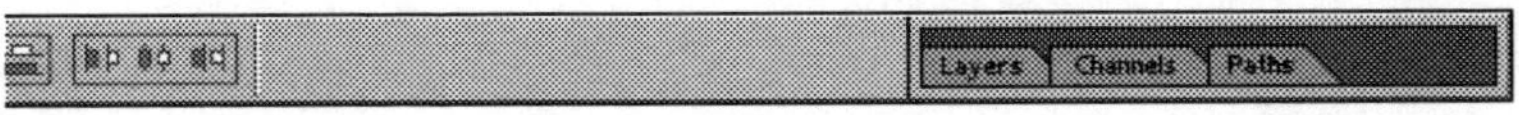

Figure 2.10 The Options bar with palette well

Separating palettes

- Click-drag tab of nested palette into blank area of document window.

Showing and hiding all palettes

- Press Tab

! If the insertion mark is in a palette field, this shortcut takes you to the next field.

Correcting mistakes

You can correct mistakes in a number of ways in Photoshop.

Undoing the last action

- Choose Undo… in the Edit menu.

Redoing the last action

- Choose Redo… in the Edit menu.

Jumping back to previous states

You can jump back to previous states during a working session by using the History palette. This palette records every change you make to an image (see Figure 2.11).

The number of states it lists is set by you, but is limited by the amount of RAM installed. Once the set limit is reached, older states are automatically removed from the list. To prevent a state from suffering this fate, make a snapshot of it.

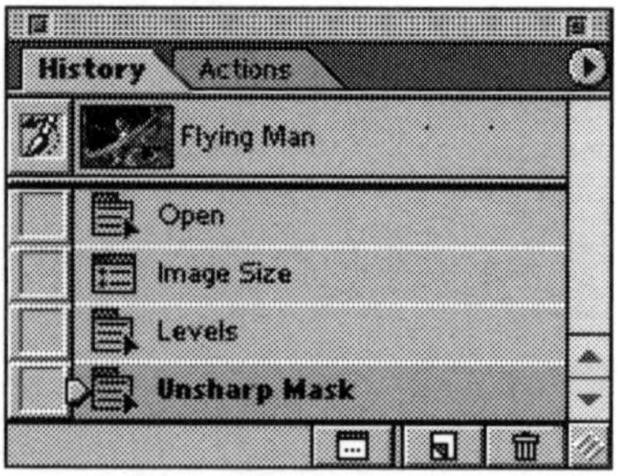

Figure 2.11 States listed in the History palette

You can work in either a linear way or a non-linear way when using the palette. If you return to an earlier state when working in a linear way, later states are dimmed. If you then make a change to the image the dimmed states are removed from the list.

However, if you return to an earlier state when working in a non-linear way, later states appear the same. If you then make a change to the image the latest state is just added to the list.

The non-linear approach allows you to 'branch off' from earlier states whilst giving you the option to return to the main 'stem' of work – provided, of course, the states have not been removed by other means.

Finally you can save any state as a completely separate document. This is the only way to preserve states once a document is closed.

Setting history options

① Choose History options… from the History palette pop-up menu.

② Enter a figure in the Number field.

③ Check Automatically Create First Snapshot for a snapshot to be created each time you open a document.

④ Check Allow Non-linear History if you wish to 'branch off' from your main 'stem' of work.

⑤ Click OK.

Jumping back to a previous state

① Select a state other than the current (lowest) state. If Non-linear History is deselected, states beneath the selected state will be dimmed.

② Make a change to the image. If Non-linear History is deselected, the greyed states will be cleared.

Deleting a state or snapshot

① Select any state.

② Click the Wastebasket button in the History palette.

▲ It's unnecessary to delete states when working in linear mode as states are automatically deleted when you jump back to an earlier state.

Creating a snapshot

① Select any state.

② Choose New Snapshot… from the History palette pop-up menu. The New Snapshot dialog box will be displayed.

③ Enter a name for the Name field.

④ Click OK.

Saving a state as a document

① Select any state.

② Choose New Document from the History palette pop-up menu. A new document window will be displayed.

③ Save the document in the normal manner.

3 OPENING AND SAVING IMAGES

Loading Photoshop

On the Macintosh

- Double-click on the Photoshop™ program icon within the Photoshop folder on your hard disk (see Figure 3.1).

! There is no need to double-click the icon on the Macintosh if it's greyed as this indicates that Photoshop is already running.

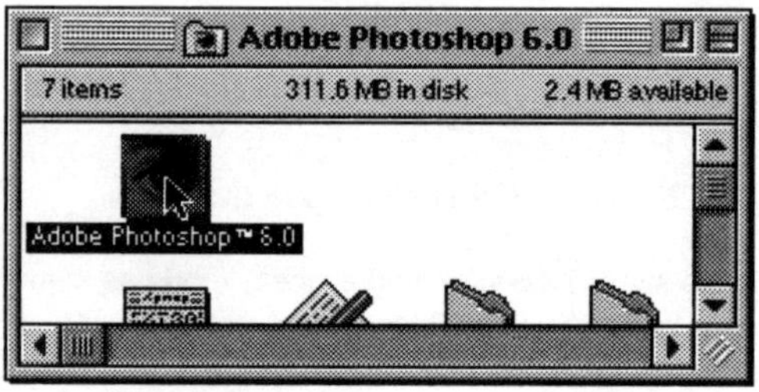

Figure 3.1 Opening a document in a folder on the Macintosh

In Windows

- Choose Photoshop from the Programs sub-menu in the Start menu at the bottom left of the screen.

  The Photoshop menu will be displayed (see Figure 3.2). A Photoshop button will be added to the task bar.

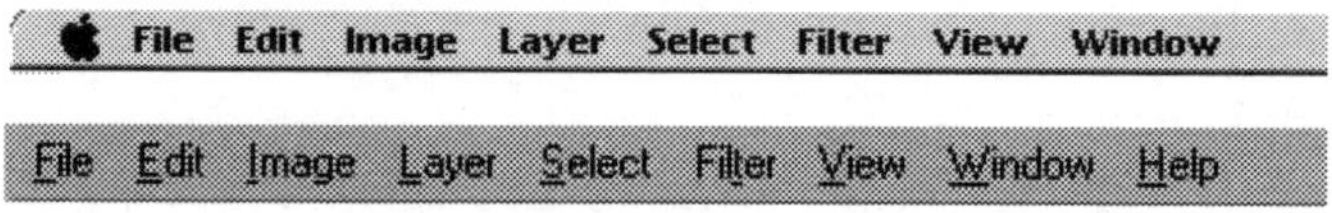

Figure 3.2 Macintosh and Windows menu bars

! See Chapter 16 if Photoshop informs you of a lack of memory.

Opening, importing and closing images

Before working in Photoshop, its best to specify your working colour spaces for colour fidelity and consistency. See Chapter 9.

Opening an image

Photoshop can open digitally captured images in many file formats, including PICT, TIFF, EPS, Photo CD and JPEG.

Either:

① Choose Open… from Photoshop's File menu. The Open directory dialog box will be displayed (see Figure 3.3).

If the Photoshop menu is not showing on the Macintosh, choose Photoshop from the Applications menu at the far right of the menu bar. In Windows, click the Photoshop button on the taskbar. If neither is present, launch Photoshop.

② Use the Directory dialog box controls to locate your image.

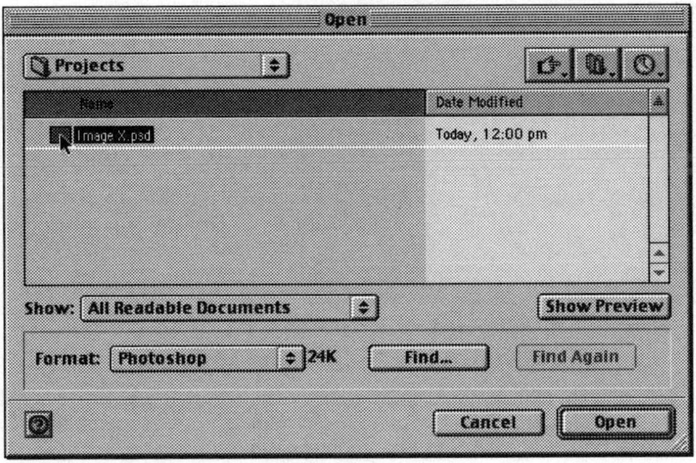

Figure 3.3 Opening a saved document

③ If an image is not listed, choose All Documents in the Show pop-up menu. In Windows, check Show all files.

④ Click Open. The document window will be displayed.

Or:

- Double-click on its document icon in its folder window, if it's already a Photoshop document. The document window will be displayed.

  If a document has a missing profile or its embedded profile differs from Photoshop's current colour settings an appropriate alert box will be displayed (see Figures 3.4 and 3.5). For documents with a missing profile assign the working RGB profile (the second radio button) and click OK.

  For documents with a profile mismatch, just click OK.

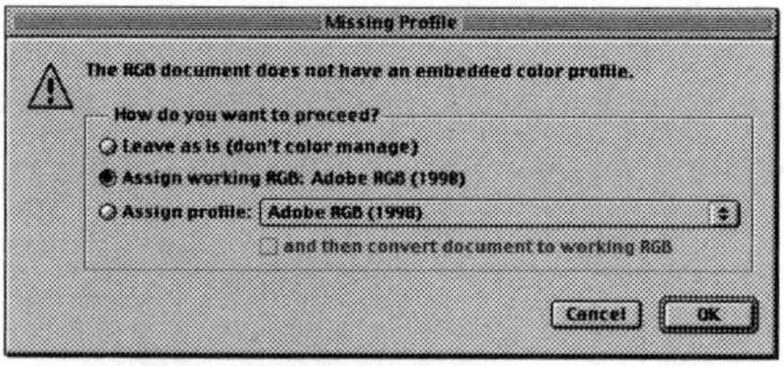

Figure 3.4 Missing Profile alert box

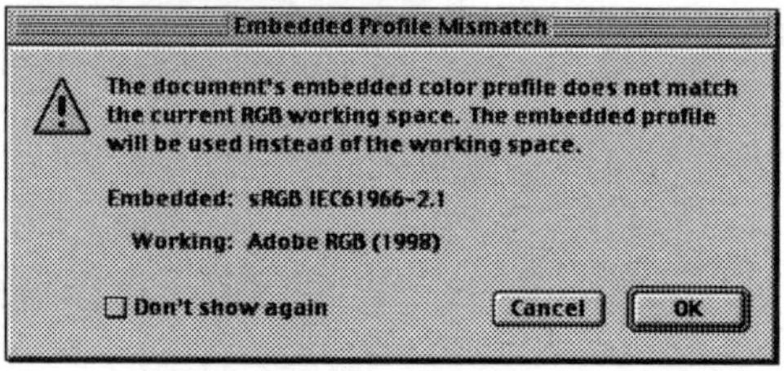

Figure 3.5 Embedded Profile Mismatch alert box

! Documents with a profile mismatch can be converted to the working RGB profile within the Convert to Profile dialog box. Choose Convert to Profile from the Mode sub-menu in the Image menu to access this dialog box.

If you are opening a Generic PDF choose which page to open and specify the rasterization options. Only open images by double-clicking the document icon if they have been previously saved within Photoshop.

✚ If Photoshop has not already been loaded on the RAM it will now be loaded. Its title and menu bar will be displayed in a few moments.

See Chapter 16 if Photoshop informs you of a lack of memory.

Importing an image

You can import digital camera images and images from Kodak Photo CDs via Plug-ins or TWAIN modules. You can also import images from PDF files.

① Choose an option from the Import sub-menu in the Photoshop's File menu. The appropriate controls will be displayed.

② Follow the procedure as laid down by the manufacturer.

! Plug-ins and TWAIN drivers need to be placed in the Import/Export folder within Photoshop's Plug-ins folder. This folder needs to be selected within the Plug-ins & Scratch Disks set of preferences for the appropriate command to be listed in the Import or Acquire sub-menu.

Closing a document

① Click the Close box at the top left of the document window.

② An alert box saying 'Save the new document "..."?' or 'Save changes to Photoshop document "..."?' will be displayed if recent work has not been saved.

③ Click Save.

Saving and resaving documents

Saving a document

Use this process to save images for the first time or to create and move to a copy of a document.

① Chose Save As... from the File menu. The Save As directory dialog box will be displayed (see Figure 3.6).

② Enter a document name, overwriting its existing name.

③ Choose an option from the Format pop-up menu.

④ Under Save, check As a Copy if you wish to create a copy of a document and uncheck or untick Layers if you wish the copy to be flattened. Options may be dimmed depending on the chosen format.

⑤ Under Colour, check Embed Colour Profile (Use Proof Setup, ICC Profile in Windows) if you wish the colour profile of the current document to be carried over into the copy.

⑥ Select a drive and folder in which to save the file.

⑦ Click Save to save the document. Click Cancel if you wish to abort the routine.

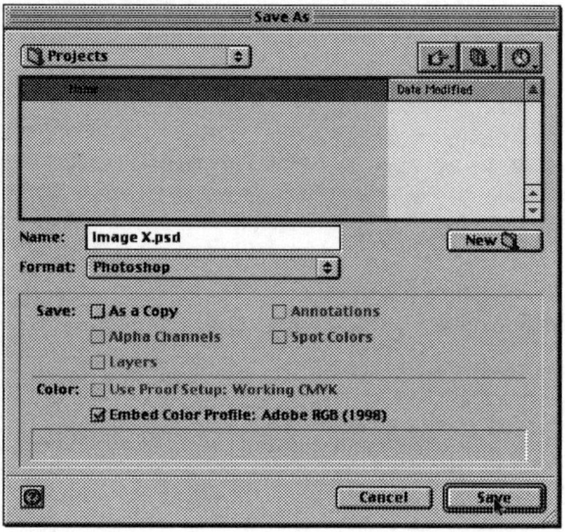

Figure 3.6 Saving an image in a folder called Projects

! If you wish a copy of a document to contain all your latest work, choose Save from the File menu first and then choose Save As…

On the Macintosh, choose Ask When Saving from the Image Previews pop-up menu and Choose Always from the Append File Extension pop-up menu in the Saving Files set of preferences.

Resaving a document

● Choose Save… from the File menu.

▲ Resave every five minutes or so whilst you are working on an image, always using the Save command. The Save As directory dialog box will only be displayed if recently made changes cannot be supported by the current file format.

Saving a sliced composite

Use this process to save sliced composites for the web.

① Choose Save Optimized As... from ImageReady's File menu. The Save Optimized As directory dialog box will be displayed (see Figure 3.7).

② Enter a document name, overwriting its existing name.

③ Choose an option from the Format pop-up menu.

④ Click Output Settings... to specify how files are created. (This optional step is for experienced web developers only.)

⑤ Select a drive and folder in which to save the file.

⑥ Click Save to save the document. Click Cancel if you wish to abort the routine.

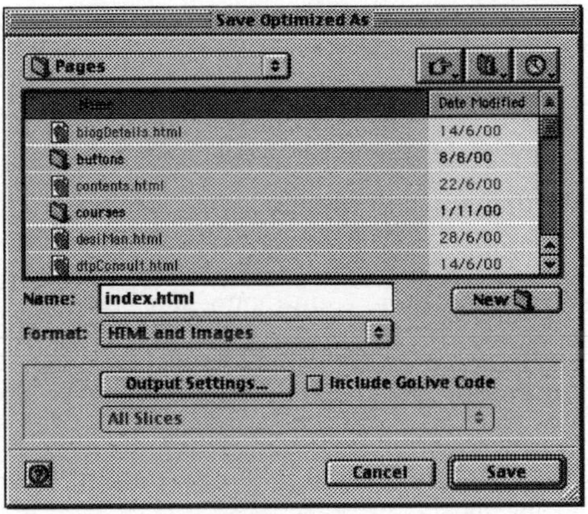

Figure 3.7 The Saved Optimized dialog box

Creating images

Creating a blank image

You can create a document with a blank canvas for image composite work or as a receptacle for a copied image. If an image is already on the Clipboard, the settings in the New dialog box will automatically match its dimensions, resolution and mode.

① Choose New… from Photoshop's File menu. The New dialog box will be displayed (see Figure 3.8).

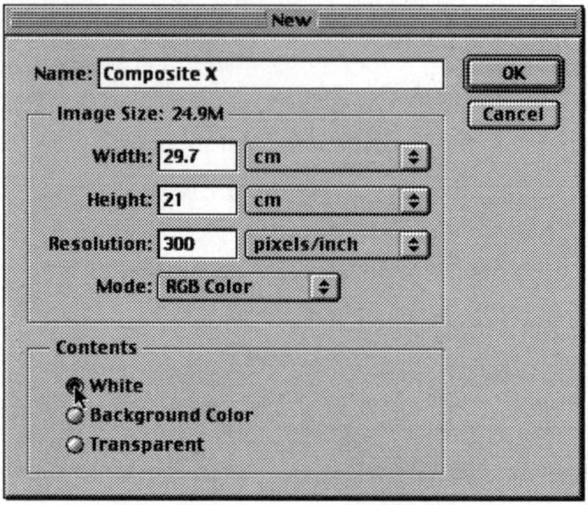

Figure 3.8 Creating a new blank document

② Enter a name in the Name field (this is optional).

③ Choose an option from the units pop-up menus.

④ Enter values into the Width and Height fields.

⑤ Choose an option from the Mode pop-up menu. For colour images, choose RGB.

⑥ Enter a value in the Resolution field. Enter 72 ppi for screen images and anything from 150 to 400 ppi for greyscale and RGB print images.

⑦ Select an option under Contents. Click Background Colour to use the current background colour. Click Transparent to create a single-layer document. (See Chapter 12.)

⑧ Click OK. The document window will be displayed.

⑨ Save the image as described earlier.

▲ When creating blank documents for web page composites, set the dimensions to one of the following: 600×300 to target a maximized browser window viewed at a monitor resolution of 640×480; 760×420 to target a maximized browser window viewed at a monitor resolution of 800×600; 955×600 to target a maximized browser window viewed at a monitor resolution of 1024×768.

Creating images from a multi-page PDF file

① Choose Multi-Page PDF to PSD… from the Automate submenu in Photoshop's File menu. The Convert Multi-Page PDF to PSD dialog box will be displayed (see Figure 3.9).

② Under Source PDF, click Choose. The Select PDF File to Convert directory dialog box will be displayed.

③ Use the directory dialog box controls to locate the file.

④ Under Page Range enter the range of pages to be imported.

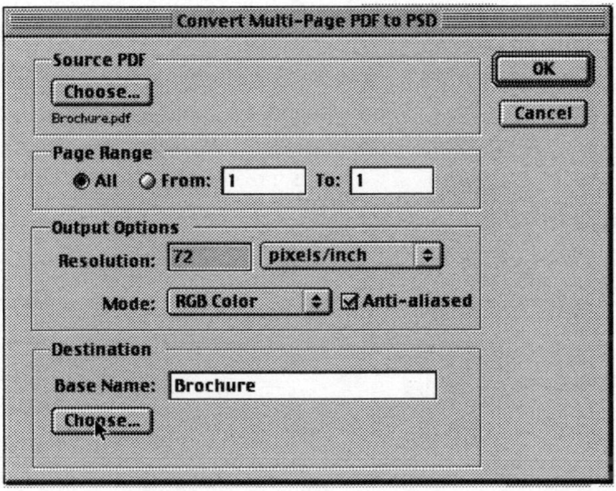

Figure 3.9 Converting a multi-page PDF file into separate Photoshop documents

⑤ Under Output Options specify a resolution, colour mode, and check Anti-aliased.

⑥ Under Destination, enter a base name for the generated files.

⑦ Under Destination, click Choose. The Destination folder directory dialog box will be displayed.

⑧ Select a drive and folder in which to save the file.

⑨ Click OK.

Quitting Photoshop

① Choose Quit from the File menu.

② An alert box saying 'Save the new document "..."?' or 'Save changes to document "..."?' will be displayed if your document is still open and recent work has not been saved.

③ Click OK.

Summary

Open non-Photoshop documents using Photoshop's Open command.

Use the Import command to open PDF and PhotoCD images and to access scanner controls.

Create blank documents for composite work by choosing Photoshop's New command.

Use the Save command before creating a copy of a document if you wish the original to include your most recent work.

Copies of documents can either be opened on saving or closed, depending on whether you select Copy or not in the Save dialog box.

4 VIEWING IMAGES AND USING GUIDES AND GRIDS

Viewing images

Viewing at different scales

Images can be viewed within Photoshop in a number of scales ranging from 0.025% to 1600% (see Figure 4.1). When you view on an Actual Pixels basis (indicated as 100% in the document window title bar) one pixel on the screen represents one pixel in an image.

When you scale up or down, the relationship between the screen and image pixels alters, e.g. 400% indicates that 16 (4×4) pixels on the screen represent one pixel in the image; 25% indicates that one pixel on the screen represents 16 (4×4) pixels in the image.

Choosing Print Size enables you to view images at approximately printed size, whatever their resolution. Choosing Actual Pixels enables you to view screen images at finished size, provided their resolution is 72 ppi. Otherwise the images will be displayed at an arbitrary size.

Figure 4.1 The same image viewed at two different scales.

Unless you are working with screen images, the scale ratio in which you happen to be working is academic. View at any scale which allows you to perform a given task with ease.

The viewing scale can be altered by using the View menu, by using the Zoom tool (with or without a modifier key), by keystrokes, by entering a percentage (%) value in the scale field in the document window or by means of the Navigator palette.

Viewing on an actual pixel basis

- Double-click the Zoom tool.

  Or:

- Choose Actual Pixels from the Zoom tool Options bar or from the View menu.

Viewing at print size

- Choose Print Size from the Zoom tool Options bar (see Figure 4.2) or the from the View menu.

Figure 4.2 Zoom tool options

Using the Zoom and keystrokes

① Select the Zoom tool (or hold down ⌘+Space) and click or click-drag within the image to increase the viewing scale.

Hold down Alt (or hold down Alt+Space) and click within the image to reduce the viewing scale.

② Reselect any other tool to deselect the Zoom tool (if selected from the toolbox).

! The keyboard shortcut is the only way you can alter the scale when a dialog box is open.

Using the Navigator palette

Choose Show Navigator from the Window menu (see Figure 4.3).

- Click the Zoom in and Zoom out buttons or click-drag the Zoom Slider to alter the scale.

Or:

- Enter a percentage (%) value in the bottom left scale field.

  Or:

- Click-drag the rectangle within the Proxy Preview Area to move around the image.

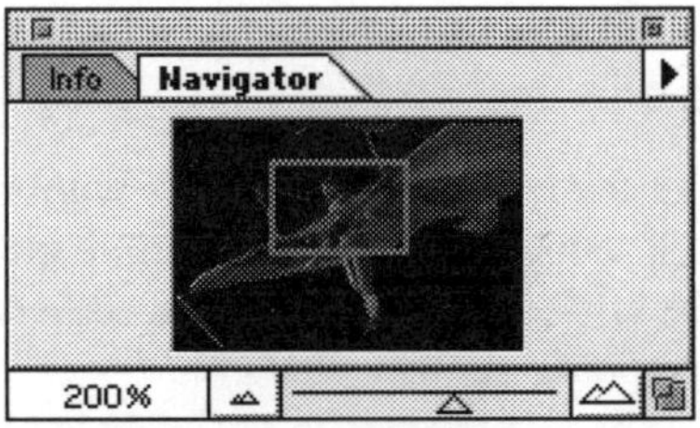

Figure 4.3 Scaling and scrolling using the Navigator palette

Viewing an image in two windows

① Open an image in the usual way.

② Choose New View… from the View menu.

Scrolling around an image

You can scroll around an image using the scroll bars, the Hand tool and by means of the Navigator palette.

Scrolling an image

- Use the scroll bars.

  Or:

- Select the Hand tool (or hold down Space) and click-drag within image.

  Or:

- Click-drag the rectangle within the Proxy Preview Area within the Navigator palette.

Showing and hiding windows and menu bars

- Click one of the the screen modes buttons at the bottom of the toolbox (see Figure 4.4).

Figure 4.4 Selecting a screen mode

Using guides and grids

Guides and grids are useful for defining the principal alignments within image composites – they are of limited value when working on single images. Guides are positioned using the cursor whilst grids are specified within the Guides and Grid set of preferences.

Altering the ruler units

Whilst the rulers can be calibrated in any one of six measurements units, their increments vary according to the current view scale so you'll see more tick marks, representing finer amounts, the closer you view. Dotted lines in each ruler constantly track the position of the cursor to assist you in accurate image positioning.

① Choose Units & Rulers… in the Preferences sub-menu in the Edit menu. The Units and Rulers set of preferences will be displayed.

② Under Units, choose an option in the Units pop-up menu (see Figure 4.5).

③ Click OK.

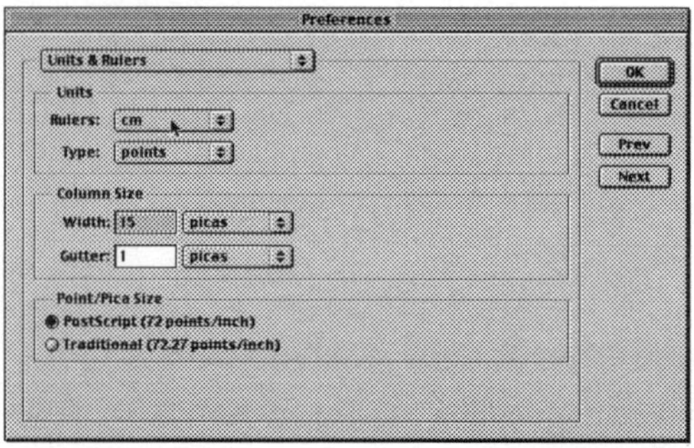

Figure 4.5 The Units & Rulers set of preferences

Showing and hiding rulers

- Choose Show Rulers from the View menu. If the rulers are already showing, the word 'Hide' will precede the command so there is no need to choose the command.

Moving the ruler zero points

The rulers normally measure from the bottom and left edges of the artboard. If you are working within a defined area of the canvas you can move the zero point to the bottom left corner of this area or to any other place of your choosing (see Figure 4.6).

① Click-drag from the small square at the junction of the rulers to a position within the artboard.

② Release the mouse button. The zero points will have moved accordingly.

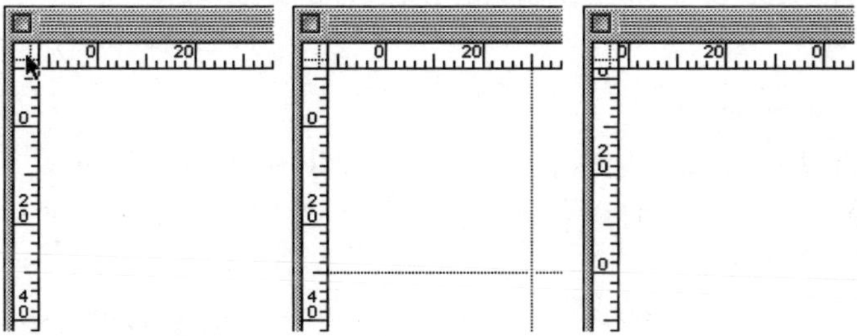

Figure 4.6 Moving the ruler zero point

▲ Double-click within the same ruler origin to return the zero points to their original position.

Working with ruler guides

These vertical and horizontal construction lines are used to define alignments within image composites and provide a basis for image slicing. They are a key aid to accurate image placement, especially when used in conjunction with Snap to Guides. This snapping feature ensures that the edges of selections are attracted to guides when they come within a two-pixels distance from them.

Setting the appearance of guides

① Choose Guides and Grid… from the Preferences sub-menu in the Edit menu. The Guides and Grid set of preferences will be displayed.

② Under Guides, choose an option from the Colour pop-up menu. The colour swatch will alter to reflect the chosen colour.

③ Choose Lines or Dashed Lines from the Style pop-up menu.

④ Click OK.

Using guides

Showing and hiding guides

- Choose Show Guides from the Guide sub-menu in the View menu. If the guides are already showing, the word 'Hide' will precede the command so there is no need to choose the command.

Adding a ruler guide

- Click-drag from somewhere in the middle of either ruler to a position within the image canvas. Release the mouse button when you have reached the desired location (see Figure 4.7).

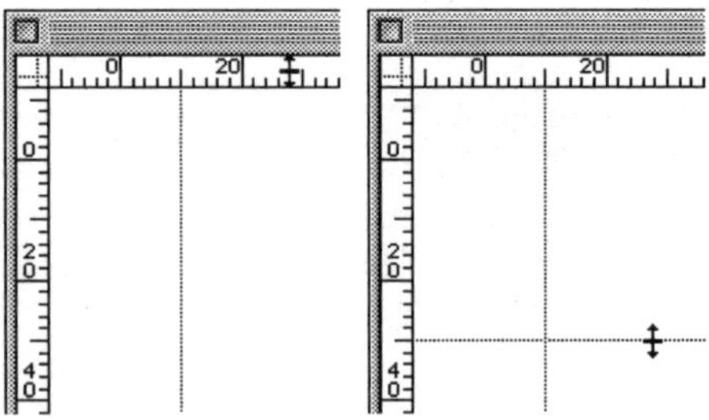

Figure 4.7 Creating ruler guides

▲ Choose a viewing scale above 200% to position guides with greater accuracy. Hold down the Shift key when you click-drag to snap the guides to the ruler calibrations.

Moving a ruler guide

- Click-drag an existing guide using the Move tool.

Altering the orientation of ruler guide

- Hold down [Alt] and click guide.

Removing a single guide

- Click-drag the guide back to the ruler using the Move tool.

Removing all guides

- Choose Clear Guides from the View menu.

Locking all guides

- Choose Lock Guides from the View menu.

Working with grids

Grids give repeated alignment points right across the image canvas, providing a modular structure in which you can position and scale images (see Figure 4.8).

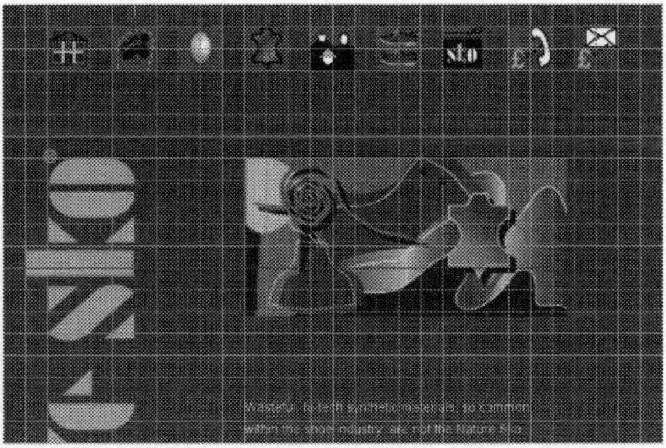

Figure 4.8 Part of a web page composite based on grid

You can choose a grid's size and appearance to suit your needs and can snap images to the nearest grid intersection by enabling Snap to Grid in the View menu. When you do this it's wise to turn off Document Bounds in the Snap-to sub-menu in the View menu.

For web work it's best to set the grid in pixels, e.g. you can specify a grid line every 72 pixels with subdivisions of 4, giving 9 pixels per subdivision.

Setting up a grid

① Choose Guides and Grid… from the Preferences sub-menu in the Edit menu. The Guides and Grid set of preferences will be displayed (see Figure 4.9).

② Under Grid, choose an option from the Colour pop-up menu. The colour swatch will alter to reflect the chosen colour.

③ Choose Lines, Dashed Lines or Dots from the Style pop-up menu.

④ Enter a value in the Gridline every field.

⑤ Enter a value in the Subdivisions field.

⑥ Click OK.

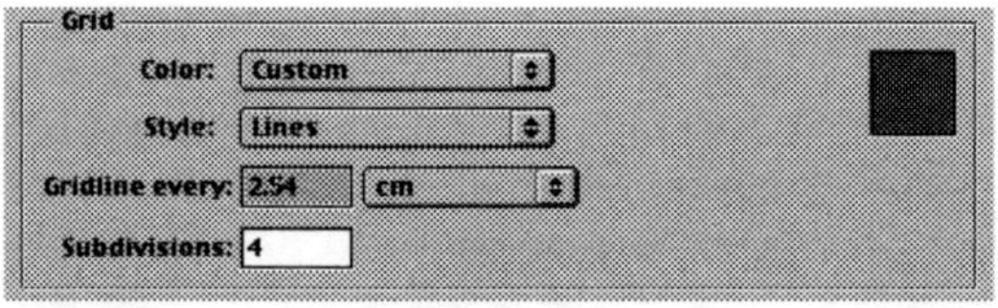

Figure 4.9 Grid preferences

Showing and hiding all non-printing elements

- Press ⌘+H

Summary

You can view at any scale that allows you to perform a given task with ease.

Ruler guides and grids enable you to accurately align and position composite images.

Guides can be used as a basis for web slices whilst grids give composites rigour and order.

All non-printing elements can be temporarily hidden by just pressing Command-H.

5 ALTERING IMAGE SIZE AND MODE

Checking image attributes

The mode of a document – whether it's greyscale or RGB for instance – is identified in the document window title bar.

Other key image attributes are listed in the Document Size panel.

- Hold down [Alt] and press the Document Size panel at the bottom left of the document window. A pop-up panel will list the width, height, number of channels and resolution of an image.

To see how big an image is in relation to standard paper size:

① Choose Page Setup from the File menu. Click A4 (for example) under Paper. Click OK.

② Press the cursor button over the area to the right of the Scale field at the bottom left of the document window. A miniature A4 page preview will be displayed, with a rectangle representing the image (see Figure 5.1).

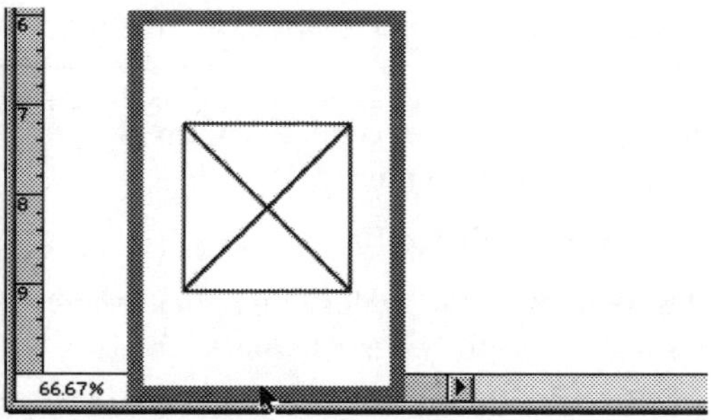

Figure 5.1 Checking the page preview

Checking the document sizes

When you add layers and/or channels to a document, its unflattened size increases. It's good idea therefore to keep an eye on such increases so that file sizes don't get out of hand and you end up being unable to save precious work to disk.

- Choose Document sizes from the pop-up menu at the bottom left of the document window. The first figure indicates the flattened size of the document (without channels and layers). The second figure indicates the size of the document complete with alpha channels and layers (see Figure 5.2).

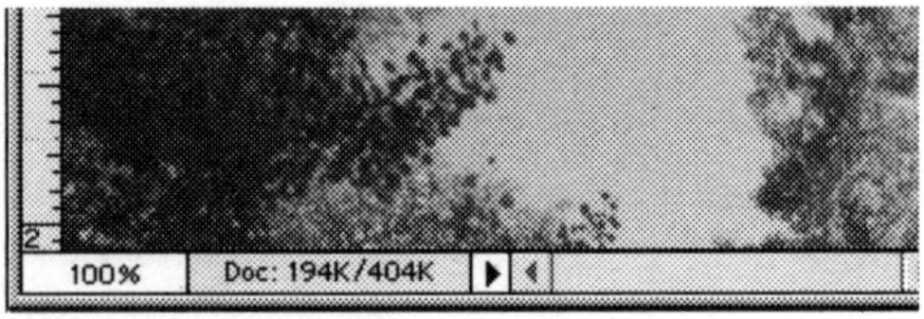

Figure 5.2 Checking the document size

Resizing images

Extending the canvas size

To give you more working area you can always extend the canvas of an image. This is especially useful when creating image composites.

① Select a current background colour. This colour will be used for the extended space (see Chapter 6 for how to select background colour.

② Choose Canvas Size… in the Image menu. The Canvas Size dialog box will be displayed (see Figure 5.3).

③ Increase the values in the Width and Height fields.

④ In the proxy at the bottom of the dialog box, click where you wish the existing image to be in relation to the extra space.

⑤ Click OK.

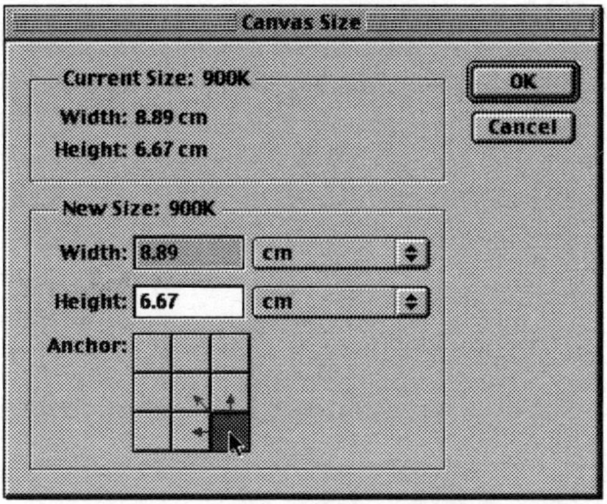

Figure 5.3 Extending the left and top sides of an image

Altering image dimensions and/or resolution

You can change the dimensions and/or resolution of an image at any time. Do this to set suitable sizes to work with and to set final production sizes.

You may, for example, receive a 10 MB image at 72 ppi. Since you intend to print the image, you will set the resolution to, say, 300 ppi, leaving the dimensions to take care of themselves. Later you may wish to resize the image to a particular width or height. Alternatively you may wish to crop the image to particular dimensions.

> ! Note that the document size refers to the amount of data in an image. This differs from the file size, which is affected by the choice of file format.

Altering the image size

① Choose Image Size… in the Image menu. The Image size dialog box will be displayed (see Figure 5.4).

② Check Constrain Proportions if you wish to maintain the image's current proportions. Check Resample Image if you wish to alter the resolution of an image independently of its dimensions and vice versa.

③ Under Document Size, enter the target resolution in the Resolution field (if Resample Image is unchecked, any alteration will affect the dimensions).

For screen images the target resolution is likely to be 72 ppi. For print images the target resolution may be anything from 150 to 400 ppi.

For print images:

④ Under Document Size, enter new values in the Width and Height fields (if Constrain Proportions is checked you need enter only one value).

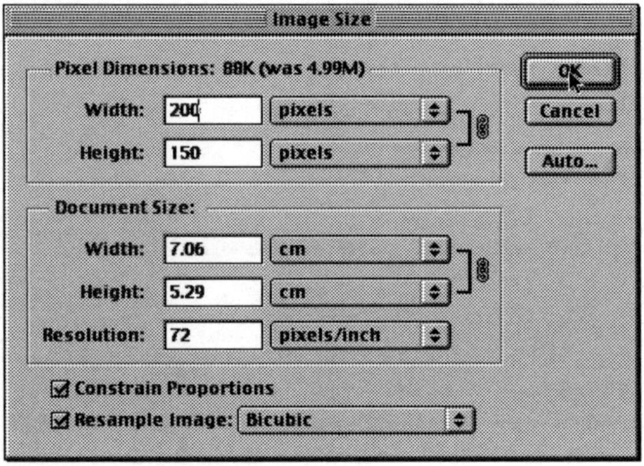

Figure 5.4 The Image Size dialog box

For screen images:

④ Under Pixel Dimensions, enter new values in the Width and Height fields (if Constrain Proportions is checked you need enter only one value).

Omit step 4 in both cases if Resample Image is unchecked and you wish the dimensions to be determined by the resolution and not the other way round.

⑤ Note the revised document size after Pixel Dimensions. The document size will be unaltered if Resample Image is unchecked.

⑥ Click OK.

If Resample Image is checked when altering the image size, resampling invariably takes place, resulting in pixels being added or deleted.

Increasing the document size results in the creation of brand-new pixels based on existing tonal/colour values. Large increases in size (four times the current size and upwards) leads to dithering on the edges of images, obvious pixelation, lack of sharpness and loss of detail.

Reducing the document size results in the removal of pixels. Extreme reductions have no detrimental visual effects, provided the resolution is appropriate for a given use.

Any resampling involves interpolation, a process of assigning colours to pixels. The method of interpolation can be altered to suit a particular image. Bicubic is best for most subjects; Nearest Neighbour is sometimes appropriate as it doesn't involve anti-alaising – no new colours are introduced as a result. The method is chosen within the pop-up menu at the bottom of the Image Size dialog box.

Cropping an image

You can crop an image freely or to a target dimension or proportion. Cropping to a fixed target size inevitably involves resampling. If the document size quadruples as a result of cropping the image definition will be severely affected (see previous section)

Recropping an image freely

① Select the Cropping tool.

② Either enter target figures in the width, height and resolution fields in the Options bar or leave blank (see Figure 5.5).

Figure 5.5 Crop tool options

③ Click-drag diagonally across an image to define the crop area (see Figure 5.6).

④ Click-drag outside the cropping area to rotate a crop.

⑤ Check Perspective if you wish to straighten out distorted images.

⑥ Click-drag corner handle of crop border to alter the crop dimensions (or crop shape, if Perspective is checked).

⑦ Press ↵ or Esc to cancel.

Figure 5.6 Cropping an image

- Cropping without target figures reduces the dimensions of an image whilst maintaining its resolution. No resampling takes place when the tool is used in this way. way

Resolution and file size

The document size of an image is determined by the number of pixels it contains. Doubling the resolution quadruples the file. Doubling its height and width does the same. So small decreases in either attribute can give you significant size reductions when required.

It goes without saying that two images can have the same document size but differ in dimensions and resolutions. For instance, a 10×10 inch (720×720 pixel) image at 72 ppi will have the same document size as a 5×5 inch (720×720 pixel) image at 144 ppi. This is usually the result of image size changes made to copies of images where resampling is not involved.

Changing the mode of images

Colour models and image modes

The mode of an image determines the model used for display and output purposes. For instance, images in RGB mode use the RGB colour model whereas images in CMYK use the CMYK model. Some modes, such as Duotone and Indexed Colour, are for specialized colour output; the former based on greyscale data, the latter on RGB data.

Colour modes affect the number of channels and thus the document size of an image. RGB images have three channels whereas CMYK has four. This means that RGB images are effectively three-quarters of the size of CMYK images. Greyscale images, being single channel, are one-third the size of equivalent RGB images.

Working with colour modes

Colour images should be worked on in RGB until final output.

There are several advantages in doing this:

- Being three-quarters the size of CMYK images they take up less memory – disk space and RAM.
- They have a broader colour gamut than CMYK images – and thus hold more data for image enhancement.
- They can form the basis for both screen and print images, since they retain their saturated colours.

Converting from one mode to another

You will wish to convert from RGB to greyscale for a number of reasons: to create single-channel 'black and white' images, and as a step to creating Bitmap and duotone images. Converting from greyscale to RGB on the other hand provides you with the opportunity to colour tint 'black and white' images using the paint tools in Colour mode or the Colourize option in the Hue/Saturation dialog box.

You only need to convert RGB images to CMYK when making colour separations (See Chapter 19). Since the colour gamut of the CMYK is smaller than that of RGB, colours that fall outside its colour space will be replaced by the nearest in-gamut colour.

Modes

Bitmap mode

Bitmap images consist of a single bi-level channel with pixels that are either black or white.

Greyscale and duotones

Monochrome images – scans of black and white photographs and suchlike – consist of a single greyscale channel with pixels at maximum strength printing solid black and at minimum strength leaving white. Intervening values give 254 levels of grey.

Duotones are essentially greyscale images printed in two colours, with one of the colours usually being black. They embody twice as many colour values as greyscale images and as a result give a richer, more subtle effect.

RGB mode

Computer devices which use light as a medium, such as scanners and monitors, employ the RGB system. It's an additive system, with its three colours – red, green and blue – at full strength producing white light and at minimum strength leaving black. Equal strengths of each colour produce grey and unequal strengths create the hues in various degrees of brightness and saturation (see Chapter 6).

Indexed colour mode

Indexed colour uses at most 256 RGB colours. When converting to indexed colour Photoshop builds a colour lookup table (CLUT), which stores and indexes the colours in the image. If the colour in the original image does not appear in the table, the program chooses the closest one or simulates the colour using available colours. By limiting the palette of colours to 256 or less, file sizes are reduced and downloading speeds increased. Since the mode doesn't support extensive editing it's necessary to convert images back to RGB for such work.

CMYK mode

Digital printing devices and conventional printing presses mostly use the four CMYK colours, known as the process colours. Unlike the RGB colour space this is a subtractive system, with its three colours – cyan, magenta, yellow – at medium strength producing near-black and all four colours at minimum strength leaving white. Black (the Key colour) is included in the model to provide a deep black not attainable by the colours alone because of impurities in inks (see Chapter 6).

Changing the mode (generally)

- Choose an option from the Mode sub-menu in the Image menu.

Changing the mode to Indexed Colour

To convert to Indexed Colour the image needs to be in RGB mode (see Chapter 15).

Changing the mode to CMYK

To convert to CMYK the image needs to be in RGB mode.

① Choose a suitable CMYK profile in the Colour Settings dialog box (see Chapter 15).

② Choose CMYK from the Mode sub-menu in the Image menu.

Changing the mode to Bitmap

To make a Bitmap image you need to start in greyscale.

① Choose Bitmap from the Mode sub-menu in the Image menu. The Bitmap dialog box will be displayed (see Figure 5.7).

② Under Resolution, enter a value in the Output field.

③ Select an option from the Method pop-up menu.

④ Click OK.

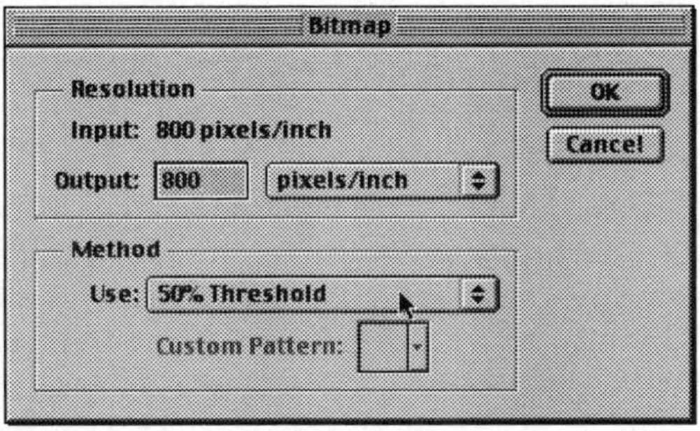

Figure 5.7 The Bitmap dialog box

Changing the mode to duotone

To make a duotone you need to start with a greyscale image.

① Choose Duotone from the Mode sub-menu in the Image menu. The Duotone Options dialog box will be displayed (see Figure 5.8).

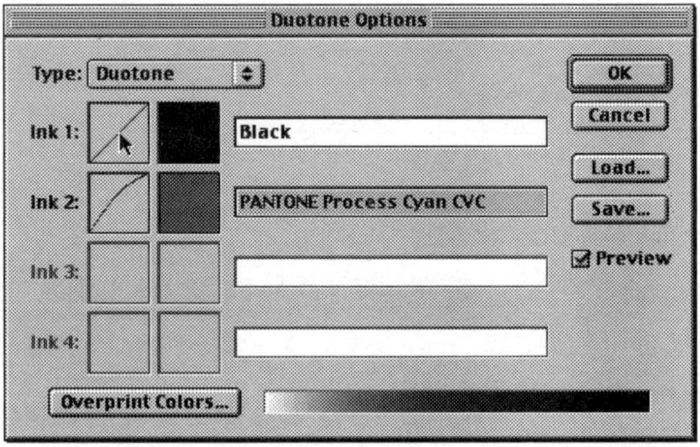

Figure 5.8 The Duotone Options dialog box

② Choose Duotone from the Type pop-up menu.

③ Click in the square beneath the black square. Choose a colour. (See Chapter 6 on the use of the Colour Picker and Custom colour dialog box.) Click OK.

④ Click in the square to the left of the colour you have chosen. The Duotone Curve dialog box will be displayed (see Figure 5.9).

⑤ Enter a value in the 50 field to alter the gamma – brightness – of the colour. Notice the effect it has on the horizontal gradient in the Duotone Options dialog box. Click OK.

⑥ Click in the square to the left of the black square and adjust its brightness. Notice the effect it has on the horizontal gradient in the Duotone Options dialog box. Click OK.

⑦ Click OK.

▲ Click Load to access Photoshop's sample duotones, if only to see the curves used for each colour.

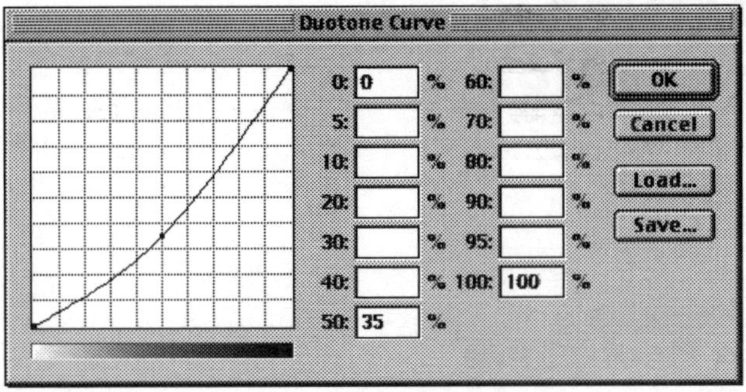

Figure 5.9 The Duotone Curve dialog box

Changing the bit-depth of RGB images

Images scanned at 48-bit (16 bits per channel) need to be converted to 24-bit (8 bits per channel) for most work. Having said this, a wide number of tools and controls can be applied to 48-bit files if you wish to benefit from the large amount of colour data that these files support.

- Choose either 8 bits/Channel or 16 bits/Channel from the Mode sub-menu in the Image menu.

Summary

You can alter the dimensions and/or resolution of an image using the Image Size controls.

Increasing the file size by more than 400% when resizing often leads to poor image quality.

You can crop an image freely or fix a target size. Cropping freely avoids image resampling whereas cropping to a target size always involves resampling.

The mode of an image determines the model used for display and output purposes. It also influences the document size.

6 PAINTING IN COLOUR

Colours in Photoshop

Although Photoshop is primarily an image editing program, it has a number of tools for painting and filling work, including the pencil, paintbrush, airbrush, gradient, eraser and paint bucket.

All of them use the so-called 'current colours'. These colours are sampled from image pixels or chosen from palettes and dialog boxes.

Photoshop supports millions, if not billions, of colours, but only two current colours are available at any one time: a foreground colour for use by the pencil, paintbrush, airbrush and paint bucket tools and a background colour for use by the eraser. The background colour is also used for canvas extensions and as a background for new documents. Either colour can be used for filling and gradient work.

Although documents are usually edited in RGB mode, current colours can be chosen from several colour spaces, including HSB, CMYK and proprietory colour libraries. To ensure they display well within browsers the choice can be restricted to those colours that are web-safe. You can also restrict colours to those which fall within the gamut of the currently selected CMYK profile.

> ! Only black and white are available in line (Bitmap) documents; 256 shades of grey are available in greyscale documents.

Choosing paint colours

Colours can be sampled, mixed, chosen and applied in a number of ways within Photoshop. Once selected, they are shown in either of two buttons in the toolbox, depending on whether they have become the current foreground or current background colour.

Two overlapping buttons in Colour palette update along with those in the toolbox to provide a basis for adjustment in the colour space of your choice.

Neither set of buttons actually stores colours. If you wish to retain colours for future use you must drag them into the Swatches palette.

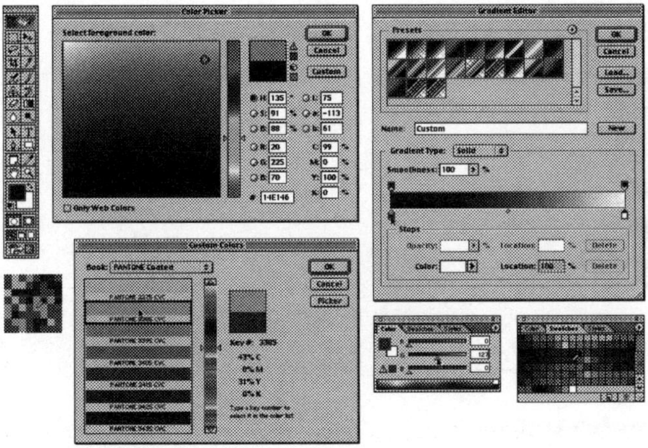

Figure 6.1 Palettes and dialog boxes involved in the painting and filling process

Altering current colours

Current colours can be altered in one of five ways:

- by sampling image pixels
- by sampling colour swatches
- by mixing colours using different colour models
- by using Photoshop's Colour Picker
- by choosing custom colours from libraries.

Whichever method you use, the resulting colours are always displayed as overlapping buttons in the Tool and Colour palettes.

It is via these overlapping buttons that Photoshop's Colour Picker and – as importantly – the custom colours is accessed.

The default colours are black (foreground) and white (background).

Sampling colours

Sampling image colours

① Select the Eyedropper tool in the toolbox.

② Click on a pixel in the image to alter the foreground colour (hold down Alt to alter the background colour) (see Figure 6.2).

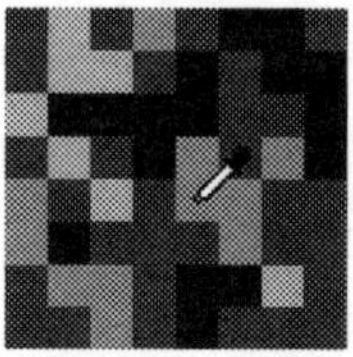

Figure 6.2 Sampling image pixel colours

▲ Alter the Eyedropper tool's sampling area for an averaged colour sampling. Choose a 3 by 3 average or 5 by 5 average in the Sample Size menu in the Eyedropper tool Options bar.

Sampling swatch colours

① Select Swatches from the Window menu. Position the cursor over one of its colours (hold down Alt to alter the background colour). The cursor turns into the eyedropper tool (see Figure 6.3).

② Press the mouse button.

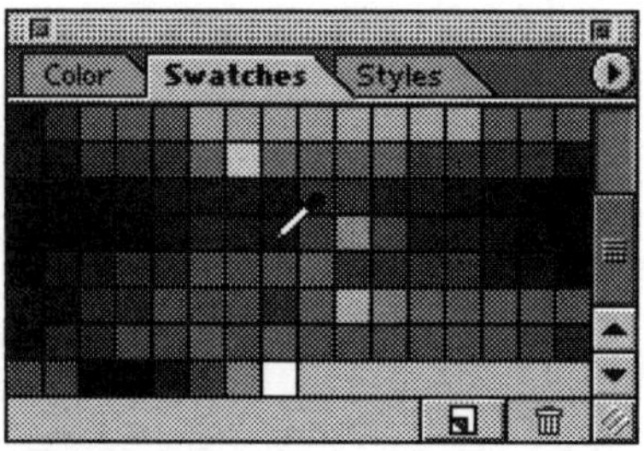

Figure 6.3 Sampling a colour in the Swatch palette

▲ You can load colours into the Swatches palette from many different colour spaces, including system colours, web-safe colours and colours from proprietory libraries.

Mixing RGB colours

Using the Colour palette

① Click either the foreground or background colour button at the top left of the palette (if the button is already outlined, there is no need to click it).

② Click a colour within the colour bar on the lower part of palette and/or click-drag the RGB sliders (see Figure 6.4).

▲ If a small triangle is displayed within the palette, the colour you have selected is 'out-of-gamut'. If you wish to bring the colour within the current CMYK colour space, click the triangle.

You can mix colours in other modes within the Colour palette. For instance, if you wish to mix CMYK colours within an RGB image, choose CMYK in the Colour palette's pop-up menu.

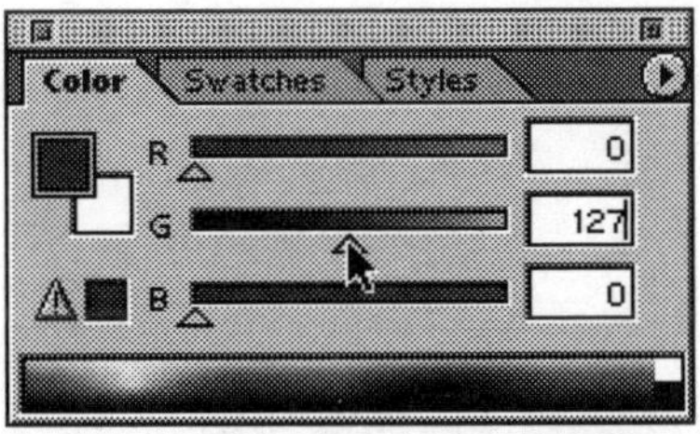

Figure 6.4 Mixing a colour. Note the Out of Gamut alert triangle

Using the Colour Picker

① Click either the foreground or background colour buttons in the toolbox or Colour palette (if the button is already outlined, there is no need to click it) (see Figure 6.5).

Figure 6.5 Accessing the Colour Picker from the toolbox

② If Custom Colours is displayed click Picker to display the Colour Picker dialog box (see Figure 6.6).

③ Check Only Web Colours to restrict the display to web-safe colours (optional step).

④ Click a colour within the vertical colour spectrum.

⑤ The area on the left side of the dialog box shows the colour at different saturation and brightness levels. At the top right-hand corner the colour is fully saturated and at full brightness; at the bottom left-hand corner it is zero saturated and lacks brightness (i.e. it's black). Click within the area to select a colour. The colour will appear in the swatch to the right of the area.

Either:

⑥ Click the Out of Gamut triangle to bring the colour within the current CMYK colour space.

Or:

Click the Non-web-safe cube to choose the nearest web-safe colour.

These actions are optional.

⑦ Click OK.

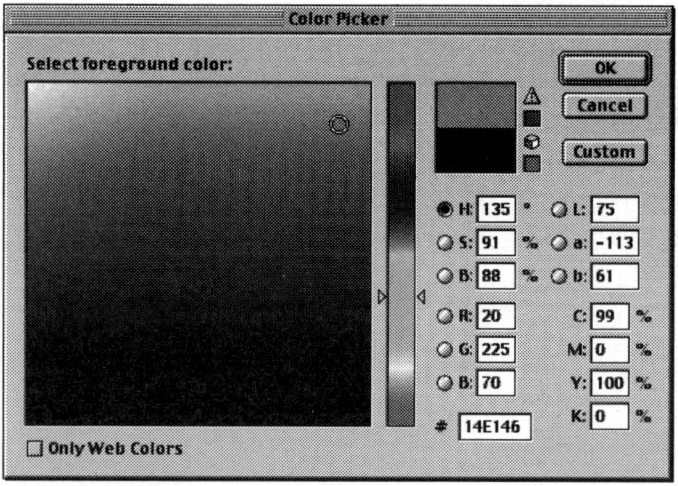

Figure 6.6 Photoshop's Colour Picker. Note the Out of Gamut alert triangle and the Non-web Safe cube

! Alert icons in the Colour palette and Photoshop Colour Picker warn you if the chosen colour is 'out-of-gamut' and therefore cannot be reproduced accurately within the current CMYK printing profile. If you wish to use the nearest in-gamut colour click the alert triangle. The non-web-safe icon in the Colour palette warns you that your chosen colour is not web-safe and may not display accurately within web browsers. If you wish to use the nearest web-safe colour click the alert cube.

Using custom colours

① Click either the foreground or the background colour button in the toolbox or Colour palette (if the button is already outlined, there is no need to click it) (see Figure 6.7).

Figure 6.7 Accessing the Custom Colours dialog box from the toolbox

② If the Colour Picker is displayed click Custom to display the Custom Colours dialog box (see Figure 6.8).

③ Choose PANTONE Coated, for example, from the Book pop-up menu.

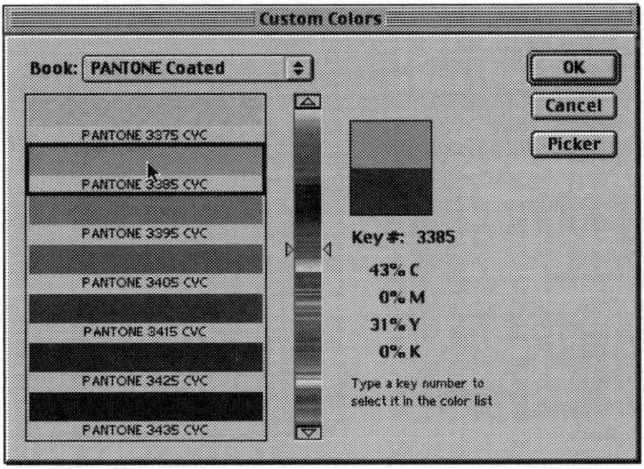

Figure 6.8 The Custom Colours dialog box displaying the Pantone Coated range

④ Select a colour by:

Either: Click-dragging the triangles along the scroll bar and then clicking a colour swatch.

Or: Typing the Pantone reference number using the keyboard.

⑤ Click OK.

Swapping and reverting colours

Swapping the current colours

- Click on the Switch Colours button (double-ended arrows) at the top right of the Current colours buttons in the toolbox.

Reverting to the default current colours

- Click on the Default Colours button at the bottom left of the Current colours buttons in the toolbox.

Saving colours

Adding the current colours to the Swatches palette

① Alter the current foreground or background colour as required.

② Hold down Shift to replace a swatch with a new colour (Alt+Shift to add a new colour). The cursor turns into the Paint bucket tool (see Figure 6.9).

③ Press the mouse button.

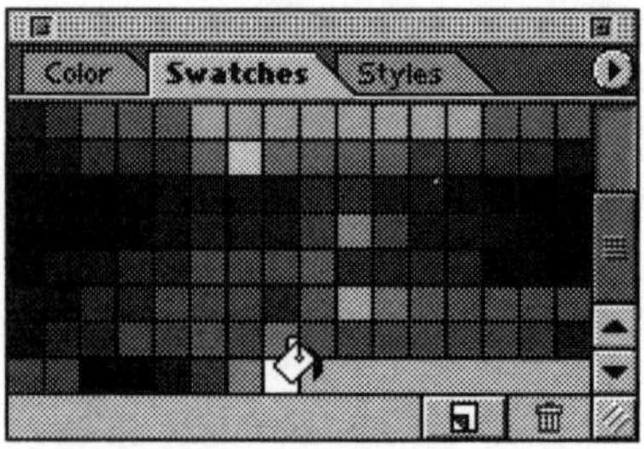

Figure 6.9 Adding a colour to the Swatches palette

Removing colours from the Swatches palette

① Position the cursor over the colour to be removed.

② Hold down [⌘]. The cursor will turn into a Scissors icon.

③ Press the mouse button.

Creating and editing gradients

Creating gradients

① Select the Gradient tool.

② Click within the area of the gradient swatch showing in the Gradient Options bar (see Figure 6.10). The Gradient Editor dialog box will be displayed (see Figure 6.11).

Figure 6.10 Gradient tool options: the gradient swatch is shown on the far left end

③ Within the Presets panel select a gradient on which you wish to base the new gradient.

④ Click New to copy the gradient.

⑤ Rename the gradient.

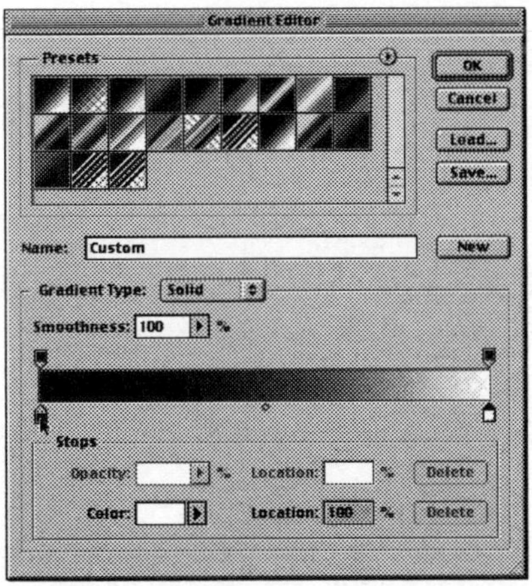

Figure 6.11 The Gradient Editor dialog box

⑥ Edit the gradient.

⑦ Click OK.

Editing a gradient

You can specify any number of colours and levels of transparency within a gradient by specifying colour and transparency stops together with mid-point positions.

The colour stops represent specific colours; the transparency stops represent specific opacities; the midpoints define where adjacent colours/opacities mix at 50% strength.

You can add transparency when you apply a gradient by entering an opacity value within the Gradient tool options bar. Opacity values entered by this means simply add to values specified within the gradients themselves (see Chapter 7 for how to apply gradients).

Selecting a gradient to edit

① Select the Gradient tool.

② Click within the area of the gradient swatch in the Gradient Options bar. The Gradient Editor dialog box will be displayed (see Figure 6.11).

③ Within the Presets panel select the gradient you wish to edit.

④ Edit the gradient.

⑤ Click OK.

Changing a colour stop

Either:

① Double-click the Colour Stop to choose a specific colour. The Colour Picker will be displayed.

② Use the Colour Picker or Customs Colour dialog box as described earlier in this chapter. Click OK.

③ Click-drag the Colour Midpoint as required.

Or:

① Choose either Foreground or Background for the Colour pop-up menu to specify a current colour. Gradients specified this way are controlled by current colour settings.

② Click-drag the Colour Midpoint as required.

Changing an opacity stop

① Click the Opacity Stop above the gradient bar.

② Enter a value in the Opacity field (see Figure 6.12).

③ Click-drag the Opacity Midpoint as required.

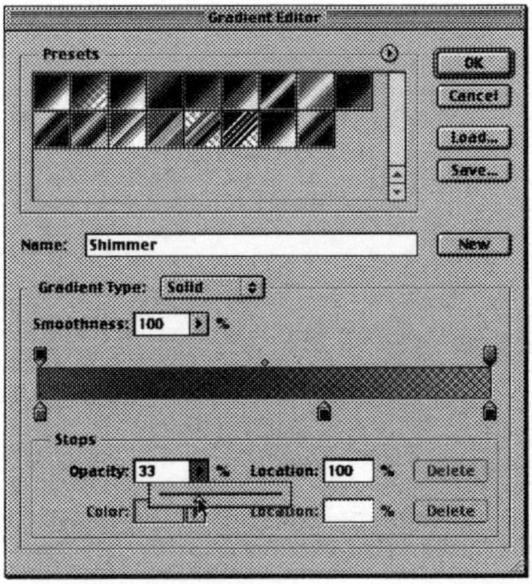

Figure 6.12 Altering the strength of an Opacity stop

Adding a stop

- Click between existing stops.

Removing a stop

- Click-drag the stop away from the gradient bar.

Deleting a gradient

① Click on the gradient in Presets panel.

② Press [Delete]

Closing the Gradient Editor

Once you have completed your editing work, click OK to close the Gradient Editor. The Gradient Picker will be updated in the Gradient Options bar.

Refer to Chapter 7 for how to apply gradients.

Using the paint and eraser tools

The Pencil, Paintbrush and Airbrush have similar options, but differ in the hardness/softness of their marks. The Pencil is hard-edged, the Paintbrush soft-edged and the Airbrush even softer.

The three eraser tools, being quite diverse in their functionality, have differing options. I cover the basic Eraser tool here. For information on the Background and Magic Erasers refer to Chapter 7.

I also cover the use of the Gradient and Paintbucket tools together with the use of the Fill command in Chapter 7.

Information on blending modes is covered at the end of Chapter 13.

Painting an image

① Select a Pencil, Paintbrush or Airbrush tool.

② Choose an appropriate option from the Brush pop-up picker in the Options bar (see Figure 6.13).

Figure 6.13 Paintbrush tool options

③ Choose a blending option from the Mode pop-up menu.

④ Enter a value in the Opacity field.

⑤ Check Wet Edges if you wish to have edge blending. In the case of the Pencil tool, check Auto Erase if you wish to paint the background colour over areas that match the current foreground colour.

⑥ Click-drag over area of image. The foreground colour blends with the image colours according to mode and opacity settings.

Erasing an image

① Select the Eraser tool.

② Choose an option from the Mode pop-up menu in the Options bar (see Figure 6.14).

③ Choose an appropriate option from the Brush pop-up picker (not available when Block mode is selected).

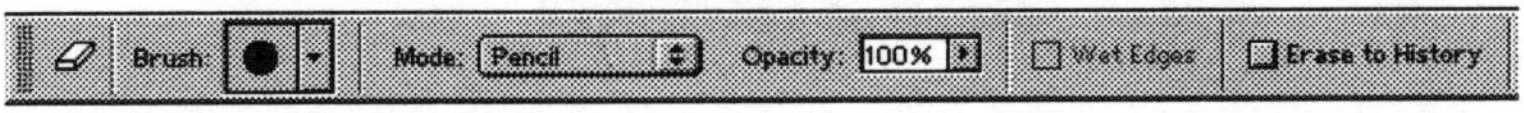

Figure 6.14 Eraser tool options

④ Enter a value in the Opacity field.

⑤ Check Wet Edges if you wish to have edge blending. In the case of the Pencil tool, check Erase to History to paint back to a history state (see Chapter 2 for the use of the History palette.

⑥ Click-drag over area of image. The background colour blends with image colours according to opacity settings, unless Erase to History is checked.

Summary

The foreground colour is used for painting, filling and stroking work; the background colour is used by the eraser and within gradients.

You can access Pantone and other proprietory colours from within the Custom Colours dialog box.

Colours can be saved in the Swatches palette to ensure colour consistency and speed of working.

You can create and save gradients for repeated use.

The brush size, opacity and mode of the paint tools can be altered.

7 SELECTING AND FILLING AREAS

Before you can edit anything other than the whole of an image – such as sky area, part of a logo, or a man's hat – you first need to select it. Once you've done this, you can copy or move the selection, distort it, apply a filter to it and so forth.

Selecting can be tricky because of the pixellated nature of raster images. Edges don't stop abruptly as in a vector graphic but are anti-aliased – they fade from one colour or tone to another. So when you are selecting subjects you need to finely gauge whether pixels should be included or not. Just being a pixel or two out can lead to unsatisfactory results.

Practice makes perfect, however. Persevere with the tools and you will soon get results that you're happy with.

Selecting mainly involves the use of the selection tools, namely the Marquee, Lasso and Magic Wand. The tools select in different ways, but the net result is the same: selected pixels – selections – are bounded by animated dashed lines called selection borders (see Figure 7.1). The areas within the borders are editable; the areas outside are not. It's as simple as that.

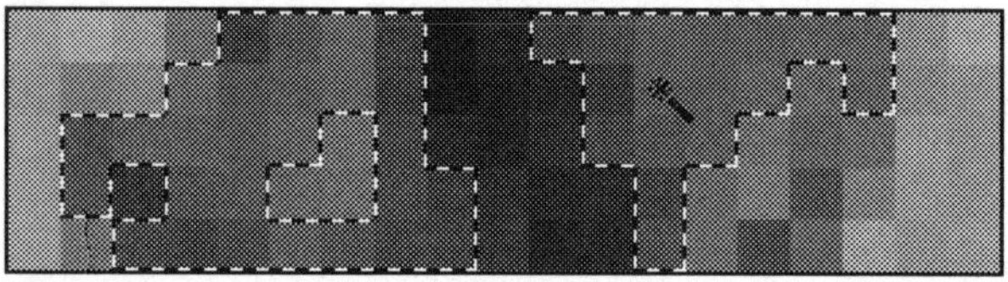

Figure 7.1 Selected pixels defined by selection borders

Selection borders can be anti-aliased or not – anti-aliasing 'smooths' the stepped effect that occurs when borders deviate from the vertical or horizontal; they can also be feather-edged. Furthermore, selections can be filled using the Fill command and its related short-cuts and selected and filled in one operation using the Paint Bucket and Magic Eraser tools or as part of an Extraction process.

Selecting areas

Selecting simple areas

You can select rectangular and elliptical areas using the Marquee tool.

① Select either Marquee tool.

② Choose an option from the Style pop-up menu in the Options bar (see Figure 7.2). Choose Normal to create an unconstrained selection. If you wish to create a selection border to certain proportions or to a certain size, choose Constrained Aspect Ratio or Fixed Size respectively and enter values in the Width and Height fields.

Figure 7.2 Marquee tool options

③ Enter a value in the Feather field if you wish to give selections a feather edge.

④ Click-drag diagonally within the image (see Figure 7.3). Hold down [Alt] to draw a selection from its centre point. Hold down [Shift] to constrain a Normal style selection border into a square or circle.

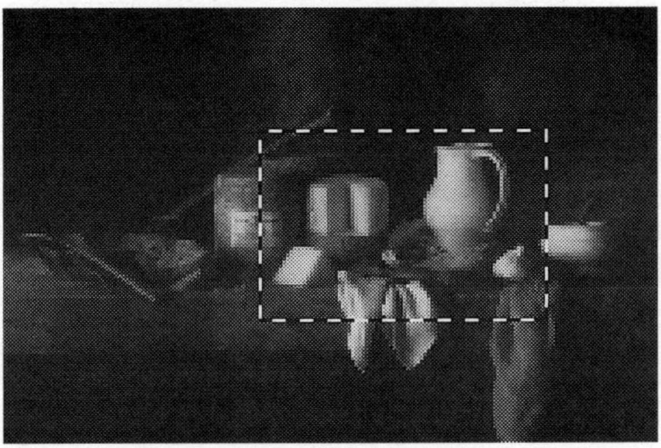

Figure 7.3 A rectangular selection border

Checking the effect of selection borders

① Select an area using the Rectangular Marquee tool.

② Select the Paintbrush tool in the toolbox.

③ In the Options bar, adjust the opacity to, say, 50%. In the Brushes pop-up picker select a suitable tip size.

④ Paint across the border of the selected area. Notice how the area within the selection border accepts the paint whilst the area outside the border remains unaffected.

Selecting freeform areas

You can select free-form areas using the Lasso tool.

Creating straight edges

① Select the Lasso tool in the toolbox.

② Check Anti-aliased in the Options bar to give selection borders smooth edges and enter a value in the Feather field to give selections a feather edge (see Figure 7.4).

Figure 7.4 Lasso tool options

③ Click-drag a shape within the image (see Figure 7.5).

To create straight edges you can switch to the Polygonal Lasso tool.

Figure 7.5 Selecting an area using the Lasso tool

④ With the mouse button held down, hold down Alt. Release the mouse button and then start clicking elsewhere.

To switch back to the Lasso tool:

⑤ With Alt still held down, hold down the mouse button, release Alt and then start click-dragging.

To complete the shape, either return to the starting point (a small circle will appear beside the cursor to denote it's over the point) or, if you are in polygon mode, just double-click.

You can also select areas using the Magnetic version of the Lasso tool. The tool, along with other magnetic tools in Photoshop, follows the edge of shapes based on width, edge contrast and frequency settings. The width setting controls how far the path of the selection edge can deviate from the cursor position, edge contrast controls whether edges are recognized or not and frequency controls the accuracy of the path.

① Select the Magnetic Lasso tool in the toolbox (see Figure 7.6).

② Check Anti-aliased in the Options bar to give selection borders smooth edges and enter a value in the Feather field to give selections a feather edge.

③ Enter values in the Width, Edge Contrast and Frequency fields.

④ Click-drag around the edge of the shape within the image. A path will be formed around the edge.

To convert the path into a selection border, either return to the starting point (a small circle will appear beside the cursor to denote it's over the point) or just double-click.

Figure 7.6 Magnetic Lasso tool options

Selecting areas of similar colour

Although the lasso tool is perfect for selecting simple well-defined shapes it's less good at selecting areas with untidy edges. Provided such areas are consistent in colouring a selection method based on colour similarity and not shape is available to you. The Magic Wand, Magic Eraser and Paint Bucket tools all make use of this approach.

The higher the tolerance level set for the tools the more colours they select. A low tolerance value, of say 20, will select pixels with values that are up to 10 on either side of the selected pixel value. Higher values select pixels containing a wider range of colours; 255 will select everything.

If you are intending to fill the resulting selection with flat colour, experiment with the Paint Bucket as it selects and paints in one operation. Otherwise use the Magic Wand tool whether you are intending to fill or not. Here I show how to use this tool. I show you how to use the Paint Bucket and Magic Eraser tools later in this chapter.

① Select the Magic Wand tool.

② Enter a value between 0 and 255 in the Tolerance field in the Options bar (see Figure 7.7). A low figure selects a narrow colour range and a high figure a wide colour range.

Figure 7.7 Magic Wand tool options

③ Check Anti-aliased if you wish to give smooth edges to selections and enter a value in the Feather field if you wish to give selections a feather edge.

④ Check Contiguous if you wish to select only those pixels which adjoin each other.

⑤ Click somewhere within the area you wish to select or fill (see Figure 7.8).

⑥ Click the Add to Selection button in the Options bar and click outside the selection to add to the selection. Alternatively click the Subtract from Selection button and click within the selection to subtract from the selection.

▲ You can alternatively add to or subtract from a selection by holding down the Shift key or the Alt key whilst clicking with the cursor (see page 62).

Figure 7.8 Selecting an area of sky using the Magic Wand tool

Creating a vignetted image

If you fill a feathered selection with a flat colour, a smooth transition will be created between the fill and bordering colours. But if you inverse the selection beforehand, the previously selected image area will be feathered.

① Create a feathered selection border.

② Inverse the selection.

③ Press [Delete]

Further selection methods

Inversing a selection

- Choose Inverse from the Select menu.

Selecting an entire image

- Choose All from the Select menu.

Deselecting all selections within an image

Either:

- Click somewhere on the image with any selection tool.

Or:

- Choose Deselect from the Select menu.

Extending and reducing selections

Adding to a selection

Either:

- Select Add to Selection in the Options bar.

Or:

- Hold down [Shift] and select the area you wish to add to the current selection(s).

Subtracting from a selection

Either:

- Select Subtract from Selection in the Options bar.

Or:

- Hold down [Alt] and select the area you wish to subtract from current selection(s).

Selecting parts of two selections

Either:

- Select Intersect with Selection in the Options bar.

Or:

- Hold down [Alt][Shift] and click-drag across one or more selected areas.

! Only works with the Marquee or Lasso tools.

Expanding and contracting selections

This technique is useful when you need to slightly increase or reduce the area of a selection border.

① Select Expand or Contract from the Modify sub-menu in the Select menu. The Expand or Contract dialog box will be displayed.

② Enter a value in the Pixels field.

③ Click OK.

Extending selections through colour

You can extend a selection border based on colour similarity using the Grow and Similar commands.

The Grow command extends the selection to pixels adjacent to a selection. The Similar command extends the selection to all pixels within an image. Both commands are controlled by the current Magic Wand tool tolerance setting.

① Select the Magic Wand tool.

② Enter a value in the Tolerance field in the Options bar.

③ Choose Grow or Similar from the Select menu.

Adjusting selection borders using the paint tools

Sometimes you will wish to soften sections of selection borders. For instance, you may wish to eliminate a background to a subject that has a profile of varying softness. This will require a selection border that combines both hard and soft edges. Whilst this can be achieved by a complicated process of selection and feathering, you can do it more directly and achieve a less mechanical effect by using the paint tools in Quick Mask mode.

In this mode unselected areas are represented by default as a reddish tint (see Figure 7.9). Modifying the tint modifies the masking effect of the selection border. It's as simple as that.

Figure 7.9 Softening the edge of a flower using the Airbrush tool

Once you have made alterations within the mask, revert back to Standard mode and the selection reverts back to an animated border.

① Make a selection in the normal way.

② Click on the Quick Mask button in the Toolbox (see Figure 7.10). Unselected areas will be tinted.

Figure 7.10 Selecting QuickMask in the toolbox

③ Use the painting tools (Paintbrush, Eraser and such like) to alter the mask. Note: this work does not affect the image itself, only the mask.

④ When you've finished, reselect the Standard Mode icon in the toolbox.

▲ You can choose a different tint colour so that it stands out more or specify the tint to denote selected areas. To do either, double-click on the Quick Mask button. The Quick Mask Options dialog box will be displayed. Click Selected Areas. Click the colour swatch if you wish to change the tint colour. Click OK.

Moving a selection border

You can move a selection border without moving its contents.

- With any of the selection tools active, click-drag from within the selection border.

Moving and duplicating selections

You can move a selection or a duplicate of a selection without using the clipboard. The selection remains floating until it's deselected.

Moving selections

① Select the Move tool (or if you have another tool selected, hold down [⌘]).

② Click-drag the selection border. The selection moves, with the current background colour taking its place.

Duplicating selections

① Select the Move tool (or if you have another tool selected, hold down ⌘).

② Hold down Alt and click-drag the selection border. A duplicate of the selection moves, leaving the original in place.

▲ Move a selection/selection area a pixel at a time by using the arrow keys on the keyboard.

Constrain the movement of selections to 45° by holding down the Shift key whilst you click-drag.

Extracting an image from its background

Sounds painful, but this process is great for creating cut-outs with transparent backgrounds. It involves highlighting the edge of images and filling the area you wish to retain with colour. The program does the rest for you. If the image is a background-only document it automatically converts it into a layer.

① Choose Extract… from the Image menu. The Extract dialog box will be displayed.

② Select the Edge Highlighter tool and enter a value in the Brush Size field. The brush should be large enough to span the width of the subject's edge.

③ Under Extraction, enter a value in the Smooth field. It's usually best to begin with zero and increase the amount only if sharp artifacts appear around the edge of the extracted image.

④ Paint around the edge of the subject (see Figure 7.11).

⑤ Select the Fill tool and click within the area you wish to keep.

⑥ Click Preview to preview the extraction.

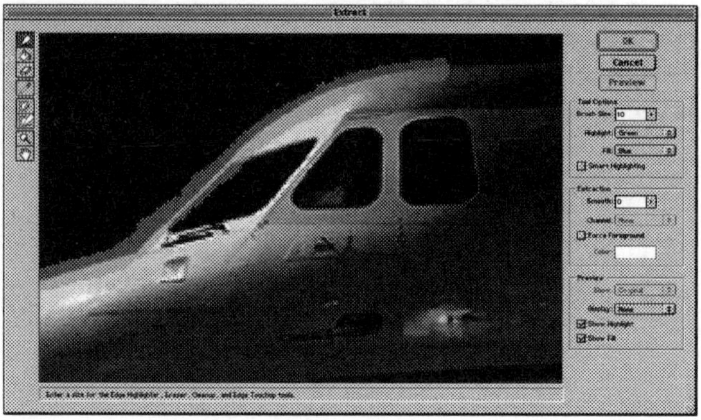

Figure 7.11 The Extract dialog box

⑦ Click OK if the extraction is successful. Otherwise hold down Alt and click Reset to repeat the process using different settings.

▲ If the extraction in preview mode appears unsatisfactory try using the Cleanup and the Edge touchup tools. The Cleanup tool allows you to erase traces of colour in the background and the Edge touchup tool allows you to edit the edge of the extraction.

Saving selection borders for later use

You can save selection borders for later use or as a precaution against losing a selection in error.

Saving an active selection border

① Click the Save Selection as Channel button in the Channels palette (see Figure 7.12).

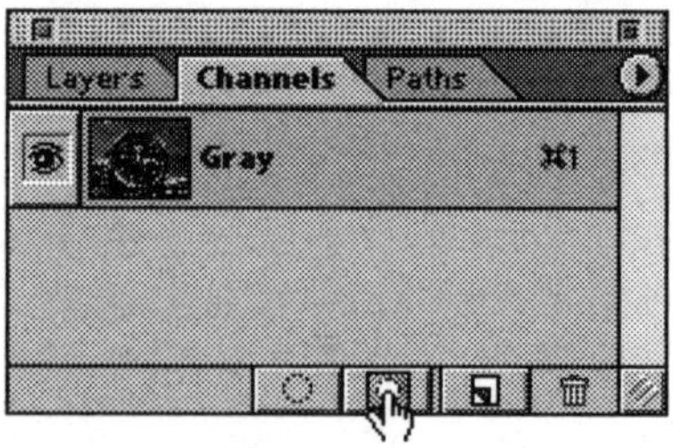

Figure 7.12 Saving a selection border

! Each saved selection adds an alpha channel to a document. Once you have finished with saved selection, remove its channel to reduce the file size of your document.

Loading a saved selection border

① Hold down [⌘] and click the alpha channel thumbnail in the Channel palette. The selection border will appear within the image (see Figure 7.13).

Figure 7.13 Loading a selection border

Removing a saved selection

① Select the alpha channel containing the selection.

② Click the Delete Current Channel button in the Channels palette.

Filling selections

Filling selections with flat colour

Either:

① Choose Fill… from the Edit menu. The Fill dialog box will be displayed (see Figure 7.14).

② Choose Foreground Colour or Background Colour from the Use pop-up menu.

③ Enter a value in the Opacity box and select an option from the Mode pop-up menu (see the end of Chapter 13).

④ Click OK.

Or:

- Press [⌘]+[Delete] to use the current background colour or [Alt]+[Delete] to use the current foreground colour.

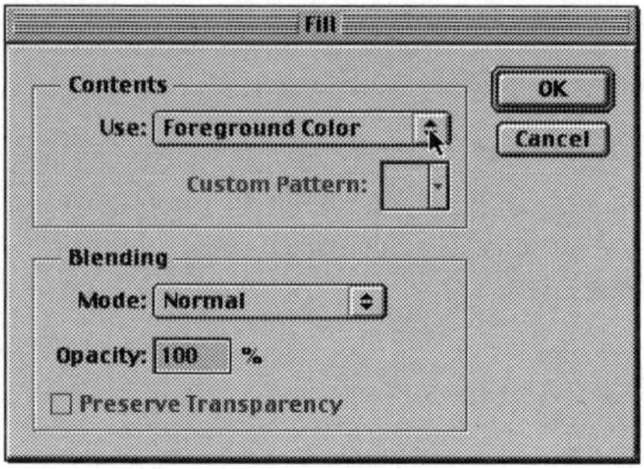

Figure 7.14 Using the Fill dialog box

Deleting areas to transparent

① Select the Background Eraser tool.

② Choose an appropriate option from the Brush pop-up picker in the Options bar (see Figure 7.15).

③ Choose an option from the Limits pop-up menu. These options control how far the erasing spreads.

④ Enter a value in the Tolerance field.

⑤ Check Protect Foreground Colour to prevent deletion of pixels that match the current foreground colour.

⑥ Choose an option from the Sampling pop-up menu. These options determine the colours being deleted. Once will delete only those pixels that match the first deleted colour whilst Contiguous will delete all colours, subject to other settings.

⑦ Click-drag over the area of image to delete to transparent. If you are working on a background it will automatically be converted to a layer.

Figure 7.15 Background Eraser tool options

Filling pixels based on colour similarity

As discussed earlier in this chapter, both the Paint Bucket and Magic Eraser tools affect areas based on colour similarly. Here I show how to use the Paint Bucket. The Magic Eraser works in a similar way but, like its sister tool the Background Eraser, it deletes areas to transparent. What options it has are shared by the Paint Bucket.

① Select the Paint Bucket tool or Magic Eraser.

② Choose options from the Fill and Mode pop-up menus (see Figure 7.16). If you choose a pattern fill choose an option from the Pattern Picker (Paint Bucket only).

③ Enter a value in the Opacity field.

④ Enter a value in the Tolerance field.

⑤ Click on area of image to paint using the current foreground colour or, in the case of the Magic Eraser, to delete to transparent.

Figure 7.16 Paint Bucket tool options

▲ Enter a low value to fill or delete pixels within a narrow tonal/colour range. Enter a high value to fill or delete pixels within a broader tonal/colour range.

Filling selections with gradated colour

① Select the part of the image you wish to fill.

② Select the Gradient tool.

③ Choose a gradient from the Gradient pop-up picker in the Options bar (see Figure 7.17).

Figure 7.17 Gradient tool options

④ Select one of five gradient types; linear, radial, angle, reflected or diamond.

⑤ Enter a value in the Opacity field. This value will combine with opacity values specified at source (within the gradient itself). This step is optional.

⑥ Check Reverse if you wish to reverse the direction of the gradient to save you click-dragging in the opposite direction yourself. This step is optional.

⑦ Uncheck Transparency if you wish to disable opacity values specified at source. This step is optional.

⑧ Position the cursor to where you wish the foreground colour to start graduating.

⑨ Uncheck Transparency if you wish to disable opacity values specified at source. This step is optional.

⑩ Click-drag within selection border to define the direction, length (or radius) of the gradient.

See Creating gradients in Chapter 6.

Summary

Use the selection tools to isolate areas for subsequent treatment.

Feather selections to give images vignetted edges.

Save complicated selection borders as a precaution against inadvertent deselection or if you wish to use them at a later date.

Alter selection borders using the paint tools in Quick Mask mode.

Fill selection borders by using the Fill command or Gradient tool.

Extract subjects from their backgrounds using the Extract command.

8 SCANNING ACCURATELY

Scanning approaches

Obtaining good scans depends on setting the correct mode, resolution and dimensions for the purpose in hand.

The mode is usually determined by the level of colour you wish to have in a final image, but not always; image dimensions depend on the size at which you wish to use an image and resolution depends on outputting or retouching factors.

Colour and tonal subjects demand a different approach to line subjects.

For the former, the correct resolution and dimensions are crucial for success. The resolution should be based on a halftone screen ruling for printed work or the standard monitor screen resolution for screen work and dimensions in both cases should be based on final image size. Graphic motifs, such as colour logos and symbols, are an exception. The resolution needs to be much higher than the level you finally plan to use as they can be more successfully retouched.

For line subjects, all three settings need to be right from the word go. Since 1-bit images tend to break up edges that are neither horizontal nor vertical, their resolution needs to be as high as possible, but no more than twice your scanner's optical resolution; so that you can tonally adjust and rotate images, their mode needs to be greyscale.

Scanning is an acquired skill. Getting good results from originals, whatever the subject, can involve much trial and error. Follow the steps in this chapter a number of times with different originals to develop your expertise but don't be too disappointed if initial scans don't immediately match up to your expectations. It takes time, experience and confidence to reach a position where you can get them right first time round.

Halftones and resolution

Continuous tone (greyscale and colour) images, by definition, contain gradations and therefore need to be 'halftoned' when output to print (see Figure 8.1). Halftoning is necessary because the most widely used printing technologies are not intrinsically tonal, i.e. areas of their printing surfaces are either fully inked or free from ink – there's no in-between condition.

Halftoning is a process whereby tonal and colour values are converted to a screen, or grid, of dots of varying sizes. The dots are usually small enough for the eye to merge them together to give a sensation of tonal and colour variety.

Halftone screens are measured in lines per inch (lpi) and can be as low as 60 lpi for greyscale images in newspapers, or as high as 200 lpi for colour images in art books. Your printing company will be able to advise you on the screen value they plan to use for your work.

The resolution of a contone (continuous tone) image needs to be roughly twice the proposed halftone screen. For example, an image which will be screened at 120 lpi needs to have a resolution of 240 ppi or thereabouts.

Figure 8.1 Close-up of a halftone screen

If you are solely outputting on a desktop printer, base the resolution on the default values used by the printer. Normally this will be around a fifth of the printer's marking resolution.

In the case of on-screen images, the resolution needs to be set at 72 ppi. This resolution is based not on any halftone screen – no halftone is involved with screen display – but on Apple's standard for monitor screens.

▲ Since die-sublimation printers don't employ a halftone screen, base the resolution on a fifth of the device's resolution.

- Halftone dots are sometimes called superpixels as they are formed by clusters of imageset dots.

Scanning tonal images

Scanning steps

① Insert the original (see Figure 8.2).

② Import the scanning program.

③ Preview the original.

④ Crop the image, ensuring that surrounding white or black areas are outside the crop area.

⑤ Base the dimensions on the largest size at which you plan to use the image.

⑥ Choose greyscale or colour.

⑦ Set the resolution to twice the targeted halftone screen or, in the case of screen images, to 72 ppi.

⑧ Set the white and black points.

⑨ Check the image size. This will be measured in MB. If it's too large for your needs set the resolution to one and a half times the targeted halftone screen (for print images only) or choose smaller image dimensions.

⑩ Choose a De-screen option, if the original is a printed item.

⑪ Scan and save the image in TIFF format.

Figure 8.2 Original image

✚ A De-screen setting will minimize the effect of the halftone screen in a scan.

Recropping the image

⑫ Re-crop the image, rotating if necessary.

The image is now ready for further treatment.

Scanning line images

Line illustrations, maps, plans, type and artwork present a special challenge to those involve in scanning. Edges in line subjects need to be sharp whatever their angle. Scans break everything up into a 'mosaic' of pixels and when edges are neither vertical nor horizontal they are aliased (stepped).

A line image therefore needs to be of a high enough resolution for the average eye not to notice its stepped edges, but not so high that it creates overlarge file sizes. Furthermore, linear detail in subjects often depends on the presence of subtle shades of grey. Line scans remove such subtleties, resulting in loss of detail.

Line images therefore need to be scanned in greyscale to give you control over how these tones are handled.

Once adjustments have been made, the scans can be converted to Bitmap mode for printing purposes.

✚ Unlike continuous tone images line images, by definition, have no tonal gradation and are therefore not 'halftoned' when output. The dots which make up the final printed image are the very same dots that an outputting device uses to print the black typematter, ranging from 300 dpi on a desktop printer to 2540 dpi on an imagesetter.

Scanning steps

① Insert an original. Place it accurately on the scanner glass, with the image square to the edges.

▲ Attach small originals to A4 sheets of paper. Use a set square to ensure an image is square to the edges of a sheet and use low-adhesive clear tape as a fixing material if you wish to avoid damaging originals in any way. Align the edge of the sheet to the rulers on the glass and make sure your image is square to the scanner.

② Load the scanning program.

③ Preview the original.

④ Loosely crop and roughly base the dimensions on the largest size at which you plan to use the image.

⑤ Choose greyscale.

⑥ Set the resolution at 600 ppi, 800 ppi or above.

⑦ Scan the image and save it in TIFF format.

! The resolution should be no more than twice your scanner's optical resolution.

Straightening the image

● Straighten the image, if it is tilting, using the Arbitrary Rotate Canvas command in the Image menu.

Removing grey values

① Choose Levels… from the Adjust sub-menu in the Image menu. The Levels dialog box will be displayed.

② Click-drag inwards the left and right triangles in the input control to 'squeeze out' the greys (see Figure 8.3).

③ Click-drag the centre triangle to enhance the linear detail (see Figure 8.3).

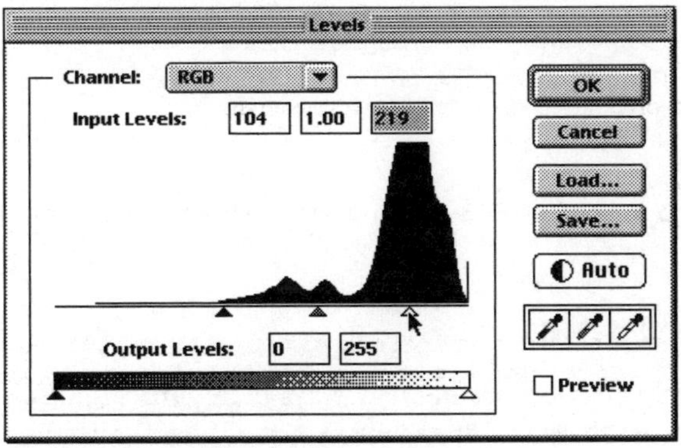

Figure 8.3 Removing greys from an image

Further steps

Either:

- Reduce the resolution to production levels if you wish to maintain the image as a high-contrast greyscale file. You may wish to do this for screen images.

Or:

① Choose Threshold… from the Adjust sub-menu in the Image menu. The Threshold dialog box will be displayed.

② Click-drag the slider to adjust the threshold (see Figure 8.4).

③ Click OK. The greyscale file will now have only two levels of grey.

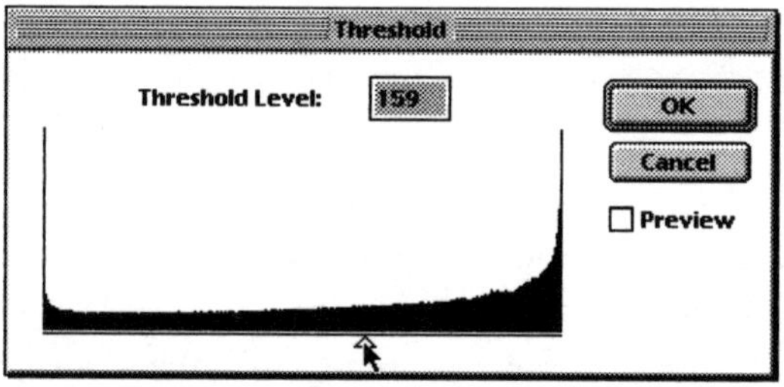

Figure 8.4 Fine-tuning line work within the Threshold dialog box

④ Choose Bitmap… from the Mode sub-menu in the Image menu. The Bitmap dialog box will be displayed (see Figure 8.5).

⑤ Select 50% Threshold.

⑥ Click OK.

⑦ Re-save.

▲ Save Bitmap images in EPS format if you wish white areas to be transparent.

Scanning graphics

Logos and other graphic devices are in many ways more difficult to scan than line subjects. Image sharpness, the maintenance of fine detail, colour accuracy – all are essential for faithful reproduction.

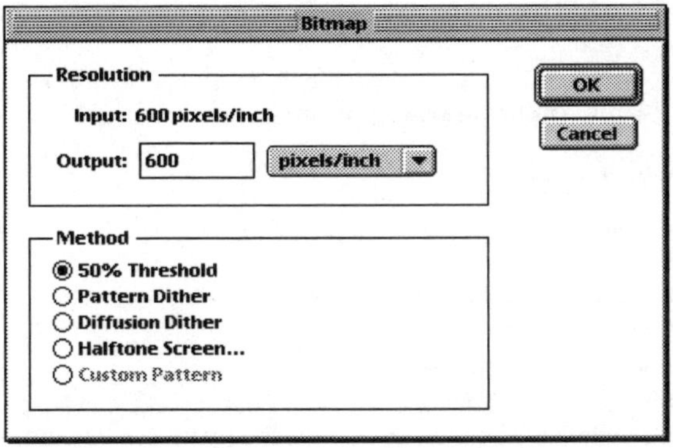

Figure 8.5 Converting from greyscale to bitmap

These properties are always more easily captured by scanning the best originals, i.e. master images that are large, sharp and accurate in every detail. Such masters can be obtained from the design consultancies who created the devices.

In the absence of a master you can always scan from corporate letterheads and marketing material; these are often more readily to hand – but bear in mind that the poorer the original the more retouching work will be involved. And the final result may still not satisfy you.

Scanning steps

① Insert an original (see Figure 8.6). Place it accurately on the scanner glass, with the logotype square to the edges.

Figure 8.6 Continuous tone original

② Load the scanning program.

③ Preview the original.

④ Loosely crop and base the dimensions on the largest planned use of the image.

⑤ Choose the 24-bit colour mode.

⑥ Set the resolution at 600 ppi.

⑦ Check the image size.

⑧ Scan and save the image in TIFF format.

▲ Attach small originals to A4 sheets of paper. Use a setsquare to ensure an image is square to the edges of a sheet and use low-adhesive clear tape as a fixing material. Butt the edge of the sheet to the rulers at the edge of the glass and ensure your image is square to the scanner.

Straightening the image

- Straighten the image, if tilting, using the Arbitrary Rotate Canvas command in the Image menu.

! If the image was scanned at lower than 600 ppi, enter 600 in the Resolution field in the Options bar and specify target sizes before using the tool.

Adjusting contrast

① Choose Levels… from the Adjust sub-menu in the Image menu. The Levels dialog box will be displayed.

② Click-drag inward the left and right triangles in the input control until the tonal contrast matches the original logotype (see Figure 8.7).

③ Click OK.

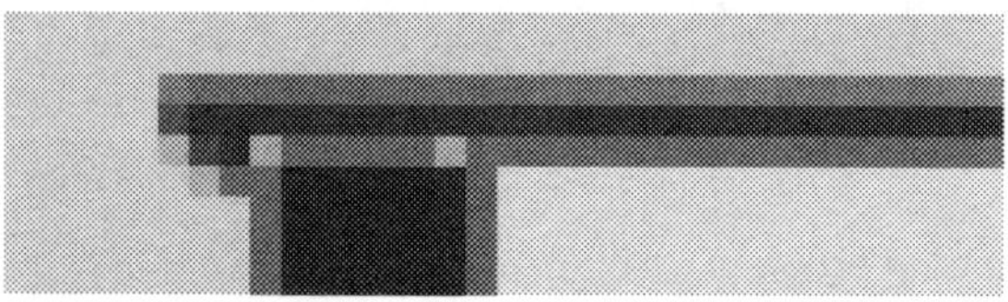

Figure 8.7 Close-up of scan showing tonal values

Retouching the image

See pages 87–88 for how to improve the look of scanned graphics.

Reducing the image resolution

① Lower the resolution to production levels.

② Resave the image.

Summary

Scan from the very best originals as no amount of editing work can make up for poor detail.

Scan continuous tone subjects at final resolutions and to finished dimensions.

Scan line subjects in greyscale at a high resolution and change the mode and resolution after making tonal adjustments.

Scan colour logotypes at a high resolution and change the resolution after retouching work is completed.

9 RETOUCHING IMAGES

Most digital images require some minor editing and retouching work before they are ready for use. Defects, scratches, scuffs and crease marks on originals, blemishes and other unwanted details in subjects: all of these imperfections may be present, and if they are they will probably need removing.

Preparing for retouching work

Setting the cursor preferences

So that you can view the size of brushes on screen, select Brush Size in the Display and Cursor set of preferences. In this setting, paint tool cursors appears as correctly sized circles instead of as icons.

Removing noise and blemishes

Removing noise

You can remove grain effects, halftone dots and other 'noises' by applying the Despeckle filter and/or the Gaussian Blur filter.

Despeckle identifies out-of-character pixels and brings their values into line with surrounding pixels. Gaussian Blur just reduces pixel contrast; out-of-character pixels become less marked as a result.

The reduction in image sharpness caused by either filter can be reinstated using the UnSharp Mask filter (see Chapter 10).

▲ High levels of 'noise' within images can best be avoided if sharpening is disabled during scanning. A halftone effect within an image can be minimized if a Descreen filter is enabled during scanning.

Because noise can vary in strength between channels (it's usually more marked in the Blue channel), it's sometimes best to apply the filters on a channel-by-channel basis. You have the option in the Gaussian Blur filter to vary the setting for each channel, depending on the strength of the noise. If you target channels in this way, remember to reselect the composite (RGB) channel before moving on.

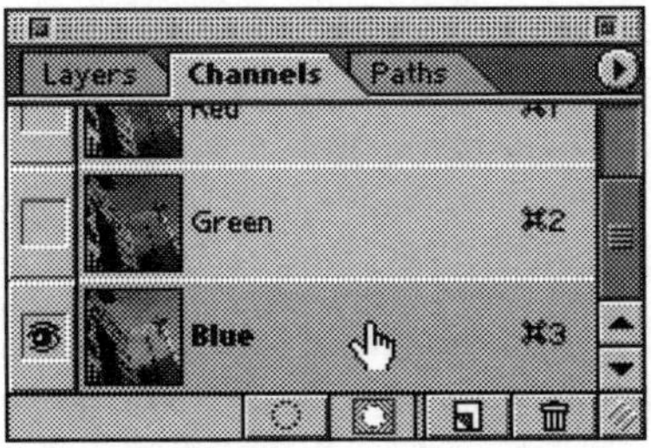

Figure 9.1 Selecting a colour channel

Either:

- Choose Despeckle… from the Noise sub-menu in the Filter menu.

Or:

① Choose Gaussian Blur… from the Blur sub-menu in the Filter menu. The Gaussian Blur dialog box will be displayed (see Figure 9.2).

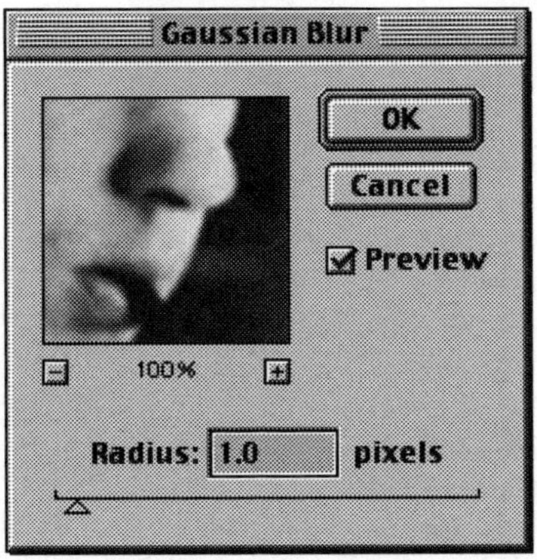

Figure 9.2 Removing noise in an image

② Click on + or – signs to enlarge or reduce the preview image.

③ Click on an area of the image in document window. The area will show in the dialog box window.

④ Drag the Radius slider to the right to reduce the noise. Keep to the smallest radius possible.

⑤ Press the preview image to view the unblurred state of the image. Alternatively uncheck Preview to view the unblurred state of the image in the document window.

⑥ Click OK.

Removing dust marks and scratches

① Choose Dust and Scratches... from the Noise sub-menu in the Filter menu. The Dust & Scratches dialog box will be displayed (see Figure 9.3).

② Click on a dusty or scratched area of the image in Document window. The area will then show in the dialog box window.

③ Click the + or – signs to enlarge or reduce the preview image.

④ Drag the Threshold slider to the left until it reads zero.

⑤ Drag the Radius slider left or right until the defects disappear. Keep to the smallest radius possible.

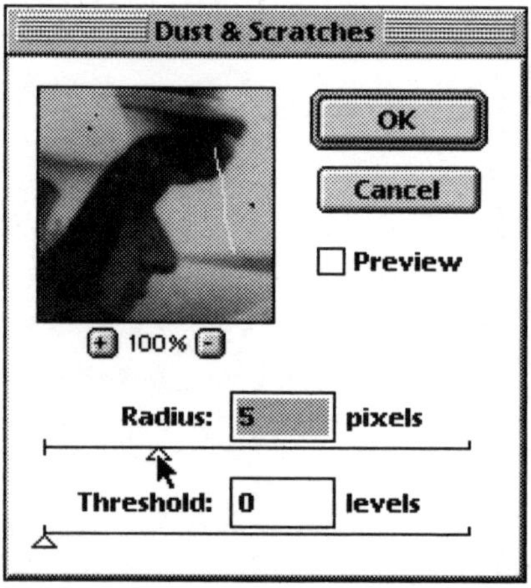

Figure 9.3 Cleaning up a dusty and scratched image

⑥ Increase the Threshold to the highest amount possible without re-displaying the defects.

⑦ Press the preview image to view the original state of the image. Alternatively, uncheck Preview to view the original state of the image in the document window.

⑧ Click OK.

▲ To avoid softening the whole image, select the individual dust marks and scratches first by using the lasso tool.

Retouching an image area by cloning

Occasionally you will wish to remove defects within an image, such as litter from a pavement or a mark from a person's face. Whilst it's possible to use the paint tools for such work, results invariably look artificial as they lay down flat colours.

To get textures absolutely right you really need to use the Clone Stamp tool. This tool copies – clones – areas you deem to be satisfactory and lays them down over areas you wish to obliterate. If handled well, the tool leaves little or no evidence of the retouching work that has been undertaken.

① Select the Clone Stamp tool.

② Uncheck Aligned in the Options bar (see Figure 9.4).

Figure 9.4 Clone Stamp tool options

③ Enter 100 in the Opacity field.

④ Find an area of the image you wish to sample. This area should contain colours/textures you wish to paint over the defective area.

⑤ Hold down Alt and click the area chosen in step 4.

⑥ Click-drag over the defect. A cross hair will appear over the previously sampled area to show you the colours that are being sampled (see Figure 9.5).

▲ When click-dragging with the Clone Stamp tool, 'stroke' across the area of the defect in one direction only as you would stroke a cat. Avoid 'scrubbing' with the tool.

Figure 9.5 Retouching an area using the Clone Stamp tool

Smudging an image area

You can sometimes use the Smudge tool effectively to cover up small defects, including traces of poor retouching work.

① Select the Smudge tool.

② Choose an appropriate option from the Brush pop-up picker in the Options bar (see Figure 9.6).

③ Enter a medium value, such as 50, in the Pressure field.

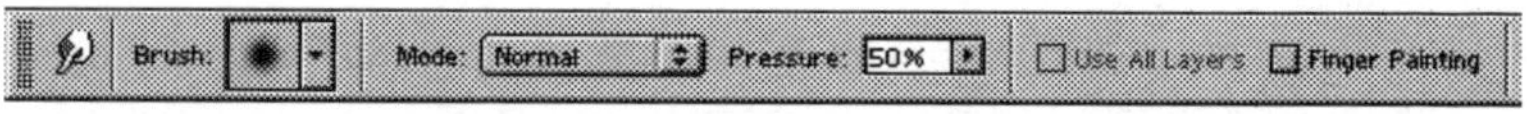

Figure 9.6 Options bar showing Smudge tool settings

④ Click-drag over the defective area within the image. The tool will push image colours in the direction of the drag.

▲ When click-dragging with the Smudge tool, smudge in one direction only. Avoid 'scrubbing' with the tool.

Tonal and focus adjustments

Blurring/sharpening an image area

Use the focus tools to blur or sharpen parts of an image.

Cut-outs of subjects of varying softness, such as bouquets of flowers, can have their soft edges re-instated using the Blur tool.

Out-of-focus images can be made to appear in focus by sharpening the odd edge. If the sharpened edges are at a similar distance from the picture plane the effect will look convincing.

Blurring/sharpening part of an image

① Select the Blur or Sharpen tool.

② Choose a tonal range from the pop-up menu in the Options bar (see Figure 9.7).

Figure 9.7 Sharpen tool options

③ Choose an appropriate option in the Brushes pop-up picker.

④ Enter a low value, such as 20, in the Pressure field.

⑤ Click-drag along the edge of a subject. Blur will progressively soften the edge. Sharpen will give more definition to the edge (see Figure 9.8).

▲ When click-dragging with the focus tools, 'stroke' across the area you wish to adjust in one direction only. Avoid 'scrubbing' with the tools.

Figure 9.8 Sharpening an edge using the Sharpen tool

Lightening/darkening an image area

You can use the toning tools to lighten or darken parts of an image. For example, shadow areas under a person's eyebrows can be lightened (dodged) to bring out more detail and pale shadow areas beneath a shirt collar can be darkened (printed in) so they don't appear so washed out.

Dodging and burning part of an image

① Select the Dodge or Burn tool.

② Choose an appropriate option from the Brush pop-up picker in the Options bar (see Figure 9.9).

Figure 9.9 Burn tool options

③ Enter a low value, such as 20, in the Exposure field.

④ Click-drag over area of image. Dodge will progressively lighten the area. Burn will progressively darken the area (see Figure 9.10).

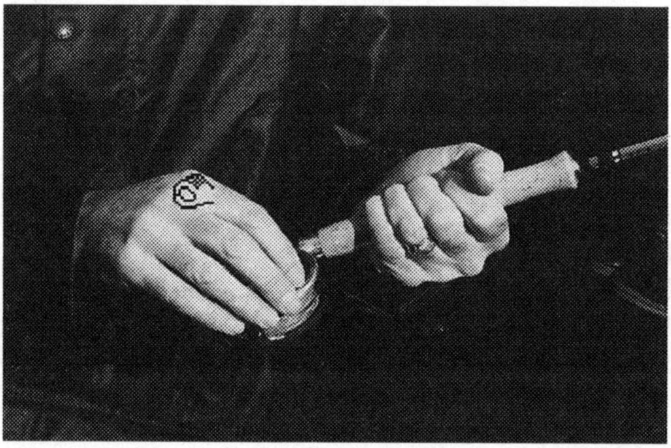

Figure 9.10 Darken a small area using the Burn tool

▲ When click-dragging with the toning tools, 'stroke' across the area you wish to adjust in one direction only. Avoid 'scrubbing' with the tools.

Erasing pixels within an image

① Select the Eraser tool.

② Choose an appropriate option from the Brush pop-up picker in the Options bar (see Figure 9.11).

Figure 9.11 Eraser tool options

③ Choose an option from the Mode pop-up menu.

④ Enter 100 in the Opacity field.

⑤ Click-drag over image. Erased areas expose the current background colour. On a layer, it creates transparent areas.

Retouching logos

Although logos differ radically in their designs, they usually have several properties in common: designs tend to be hard-edged, colours flat (matching Pantone or CMYK specifications) and backgrounds transparent or white.

These properties are often degraded in scans and need somehow to be re-established.

If transparency is important, this can be achieved in a number of ways, depending on the final medium. For multimedia images, it's achieved by using ink effect controls within authoring programs, such as Macromedia Director. For web images, it's achieved when images are optimized. For printed images, it's achieved through the use of clipping paths, unless images are in black and white only, in which case whites can be specified as transparent if the document is saved in EPS format.

Retouching steps

The following steps are presented as a general guide only. Step-by-step instructions on how you use the Adjust controls, filters and tools are covered elsewhere in this book. See Chapter 8 for how to get the best scans from logos.

Removing halftone screen

Skip this step if a screen pattern is not present.

- Apply the Despeckle or Gaussian Blur filter.

Improving tonal values

Complete these two steps for all logos with white backgrounds.

① Make the background white by setting the white point within the Levels control.

② Adjust tonal contrast to match the original within the Levels control.

Recolouring individual pixels

① Use the Pencil or Paint brush tool set to a small brush size.

② Use the Eraser tool to a small brush size to erase individual pixels to white.

Replacing both tones and colours (option 1)

① Select the Magic Wand tool and set it to a low tolerance value with Anti-aliased checked.

② Select coloured areas using the tool. The selection border should nearly reach the edges of existing shapes. If it doesn't, reset the tolerance and reselect the area, repeating the process until until the selection border is correct.

③ Set the current background colour to match the logo colour.

④ Fill the selection. The fill should spread out to fully cover the colour shape. It should have a slightly vignetted edge.

Retaining tones and replacing colours (option 2)

① Choose Desaturate from the Adjust sub-menu in the Image menu. This removes all traces of colour but keeps the tones.

② Select the Magic Wand tool and set it to a low tolerance value with Anti-aliased unchecked.

③ Select individual tonal shapes using the tool. The selection border should reach the edges of shapes. If it doesn't, reset the tolerance and reselect the area, repeating until the selection border is correct.

④ Set the current background colour to match the logo colour.

⑤ Fill the selection with the mode set to colour. The fill will colour the existing tone.

Reducing the resolution

① Save the image and make a copy under a different name.

② Lower the resolution to production levels. The drop in resolution will further tidy up edge detail.

Correcting poor retouching

It's easy to make mistakes when retouching, particularly when you are new to the tools. Setting the wrong brush size or exposure; applying a tool incorrectly – all these actions can easily lead to poor results. There's also a tendency to over-retouch, even amongst professionals.

Fortunately the History Brush allows you to paint back areas to how they were before any retouching took place, giving you the chance to start all over again.

Painting back to a previous state

① Show the History palette.

② Set the source of the History Brush by clicking to the left of the state to which you wish to paint back.

③ Select the History Brush tool in the toolbox.

④ Choose an appropriate option from the Brush pop-up picker in the Options bar (see Figure 9.12).

Figure 9.12 History Brush options

⑤ Enter 100 in the Opacity field.

⑥ Paint over the problem area within the image.

Summary

You can remove noise with the Despeckle and Gaussian Blur filters and fine defects with the Dust and Scratches filter.

Sharpness and brightness levels can be altered locally using the focus and toning tools.

You can remove unwanted details using the Clone Stamp tool.

Poor retouching work can be corrected using the History Brush.

Logos can be improved using one of two well-tried processes.

10 ENHANCING IMAGES

Images often need tonal, colour and focusing correction to match them to originals or to conform to a vision of how they should look. Correction facilities are built into most desktop scanning programs, enabling adjustments to be made during the scanning process. Most people, however, prefer to make adjustments after images have been scanned. The separation of the two processes makes better use of your time and enables you to use Photoshop's own interactive controls.

Image problems can be categorized as being tone, colour or noise/sharpness related. (I deal with noise-related problems in Chapter 9.)

Image deficiencies

Tone related

Wrong brightness Images appear bleached out (tones too light) or too sooty (tones too dark).

Poor contrast Images appear too flat (tones not differentiated enough) or too contrasty (tones mainly restricted to darks and lights).

Colour related

Unbalanced Images have a colour cast – too much red or yellow, for instance.

Impure colours Primaries appear impure – yellows, for example, can have too much cyan in them, making them look dirty.

Incorrectly saturated Colours appear weak and washed out – too grey – or over-rich and artificial.

Focus related

Wrong sharpness Images are too blurred (image unsharp).

Resolution

Raster images are formed by a rectangular grid of pixels, with each pixel representing a tone or colour. The resolution of an image is measured in pixels per (linear) inch and can be as low as 72 ppi for on-screen images and as high as 1270 for line (Bitmap) images.

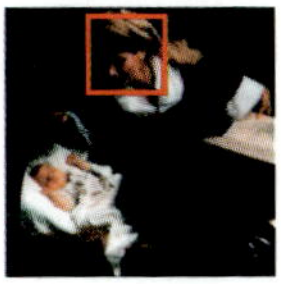

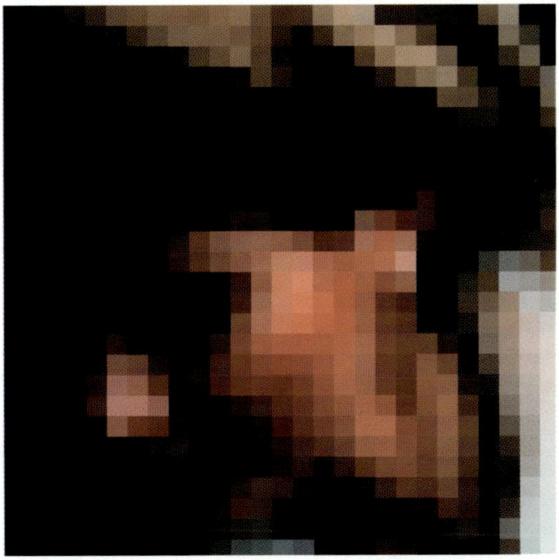

Bit depth

The bit depth of an image determines the number of greys/colours it supports. Full-colour images usually start off in 24- or 48-bit but are mostly edited in 24-bit. 24-bit images give you millions of colours ($2^{24} = 2^8 \times 2^8 \times 2^8 = 16.7+$ million).
'Black and white' – greyscale – images are 8-bit, giving 256 levels of grey ($2^8 = 2 \times 2 \times 2 \times 2 \times 2 \times 2 \times 2 \times 2 = 256$), whereas line images (termed Bitmap in Photoshop) are 1-bit, giving you black and white only ($2^1 = 2$).

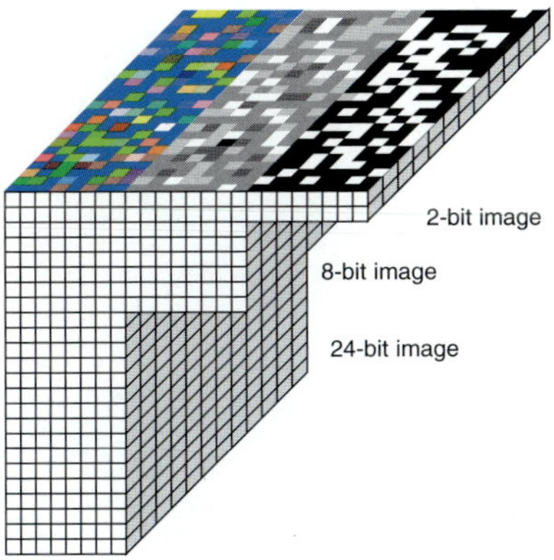

This graphic representation of bit-depth clearly shows that the higher the bit-depth the larger the document size will be

Optimized images

Web images are optimized to facilitate fast downloading times. Optimization often involves reducing the bit-depth of images from 24-bit to 8-bit or less. In the process pixels are assigned colours from a fixed palette, such as a system or web palette, or from a sub-set of colours present in the image.
If colours appear flat as a result dithering can be introduced to give the effect of modelling.

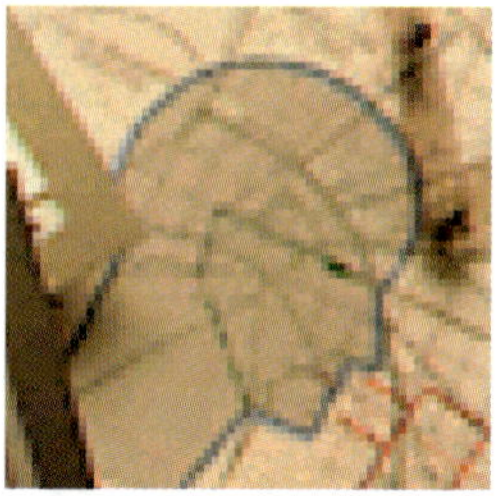

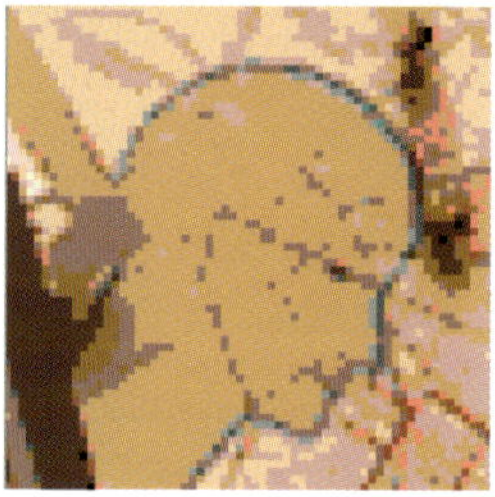

JPEG, 24-bit (top). GIF, 16 cols, web palette (above)

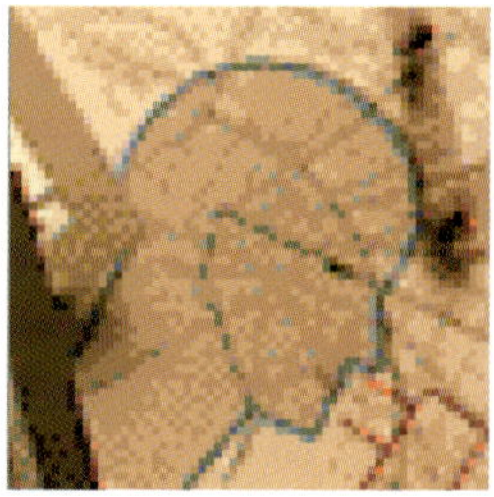

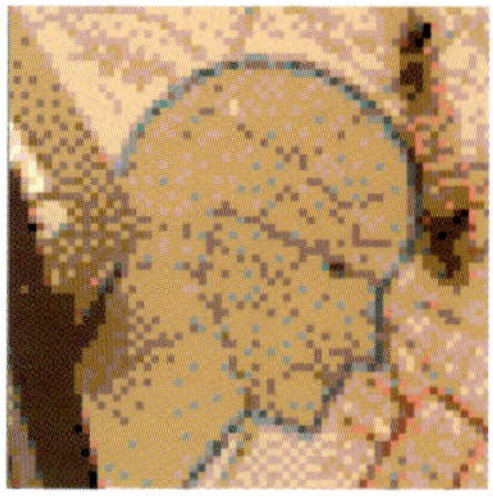

GIF, 32 cols, selective palette, (top). GIF, 16 colours, web palette, 80% dither (above)

RGB and CMYK

The additive primaries – red, green and blue (RGB) – form the basis for image capturing and screen display. When colours are printed, however, the subtractive primaries – cyan, magenta, yellow and black (CMYK) – are used. Unlike the additive colours, which are emitted by light, the subtractive colours absorb light.

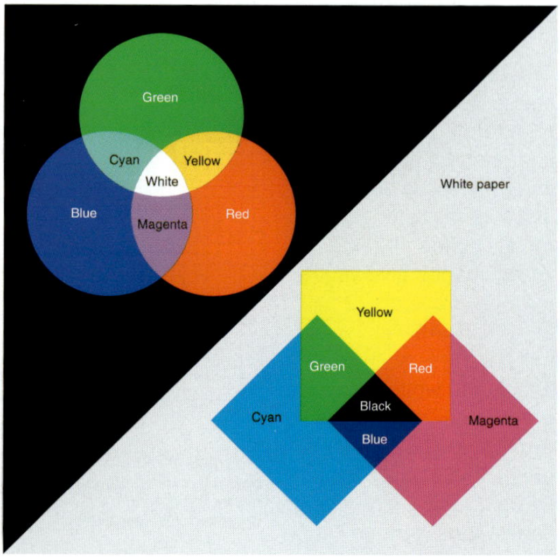

In the RGB system the three primaries in combination produce white light and the absence of colours leaves black

In the CMYK system, the three primaries C, M and Y theoretically produce a near black. Black (K) is added to give a true black

Colour balance

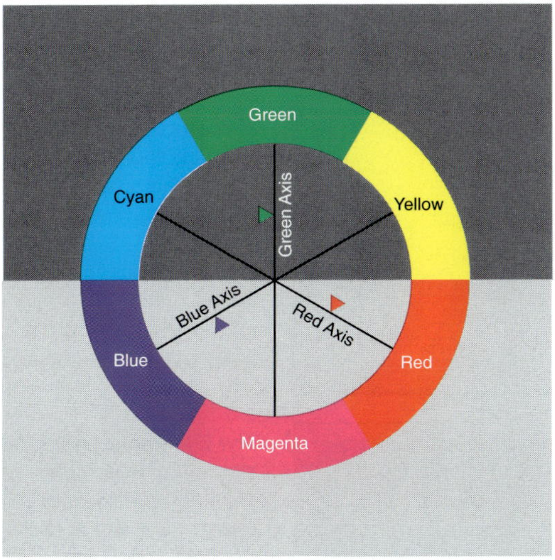

Colour axes

Each additive colour has a complementary colour corresponding to one of the subtractive colours. Colour casts are removed by altering the balance between these colours (shown connected by lines in the diagram). Usually more than one additive primary needs to be adjusted as casts may not be a pure colour, e.g. an orange cast will involve both the Red and Blue axes.

Colour bias

Correctly balanced image surrounded by versions with a marked colour imbalance. They are arranged in the same relationship as the above diagram.

Specifying colours

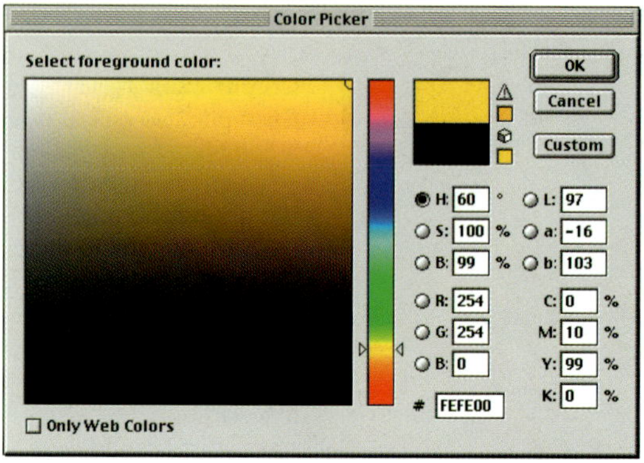

Photoshop's Colour Picker allows you to choose colours from one of four colour spaces: HSB, RGB, L*a*b* and CMYK (left)

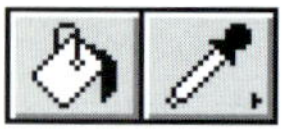

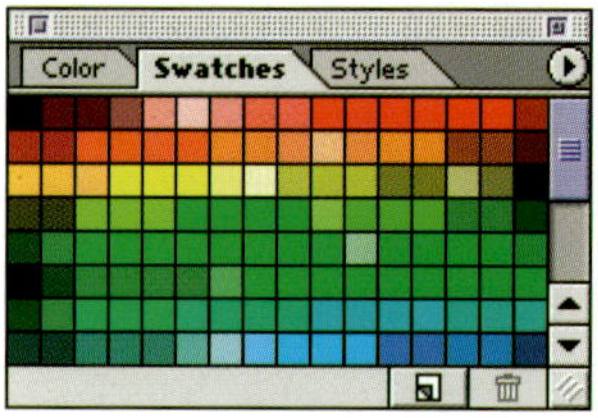

You can choose colours from a number of print and web palettes in the Swatches palette (below left).

The Eyedropper (far left) allows you to sample colours from pixels in an image; the Paint bucket fills areas of similar colour based on a tolerance setting.

Halftones

When colour images are output for print, their pixel data (right) is translated into a grid or screen of halftone dots (far right). The size of the individual dots corresponds to the strength of the component colour in the image. The set of four screens created for CMYK printing share a common pitch – the number of lines (of dots) per inch – but differ in their angle to avoid the presence of moiré patterns.

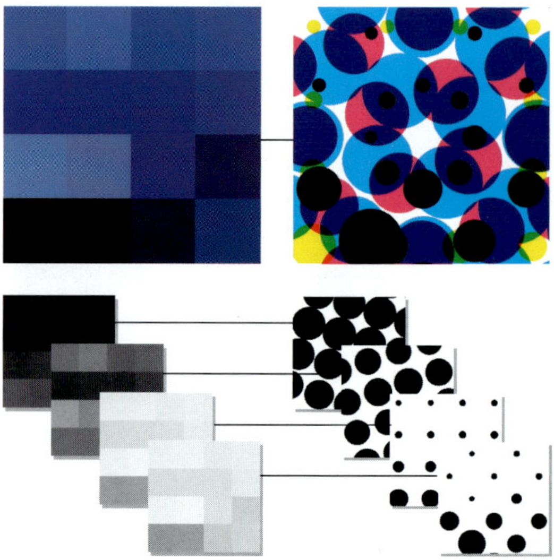

Separations

Colours need to be specified as CMYK, Hexachrome or spot to print on conventional presses.

They can then be split into their component colours to create film separations for each ink.

Printers use these separations to image printing plates used on presses.

Composite CMYK image (above).

Component colours separated out (right).

Colour settings

The monitor RGB, the working RGB, CMYK and greyscale colour spaces all need to be correctly set for colour consistency and fidelity throughout the work flow.

Monitor gamma and white point adjustment is usually made using the Adobe Gamma utility.

Scanner, monitor and printing profiles supplied by the manufacturers of the devices are selected as default profiles in the ColorSync control panel.

The working colour space profiles are set up in Photoshop's Colour Settings dialog box. Within this box you choose from a number of print and web settings, all of which can be customised to suit.

Furthermore you can specify working profiles to be embedded within files or not, and, if so, whether they are preserved or converted to alternative working spaces on opening.

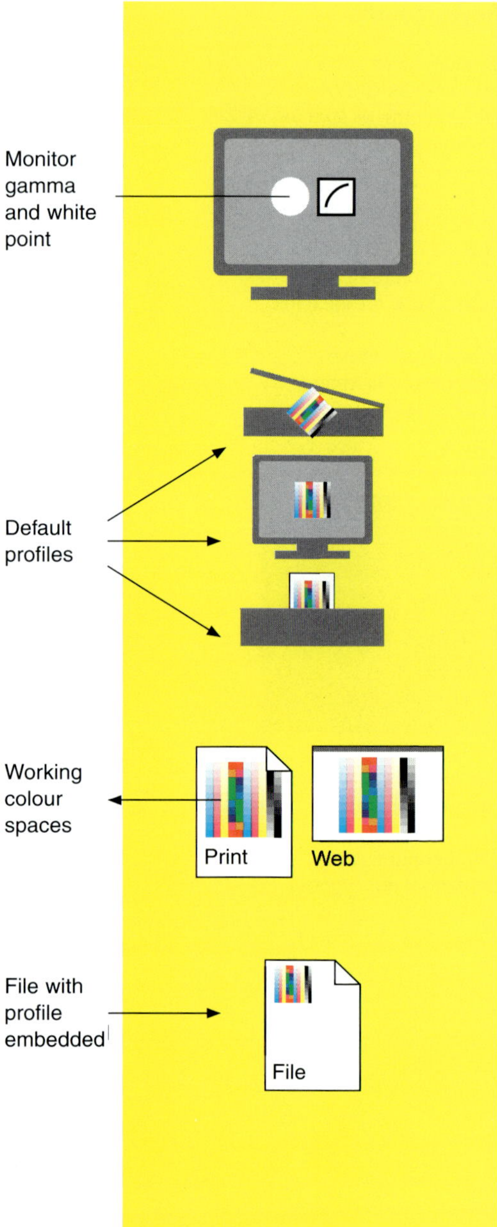

Gamma correction

Computers think of light and dark in a linear way whereas humans think of light and dark in a logarithmic way, with darker shades being compressed. Here is an example of a gamma adjustment in the context of the monitor display. It shows how the monitor gamma can be adjusted to display tones as they appear to the human eye.

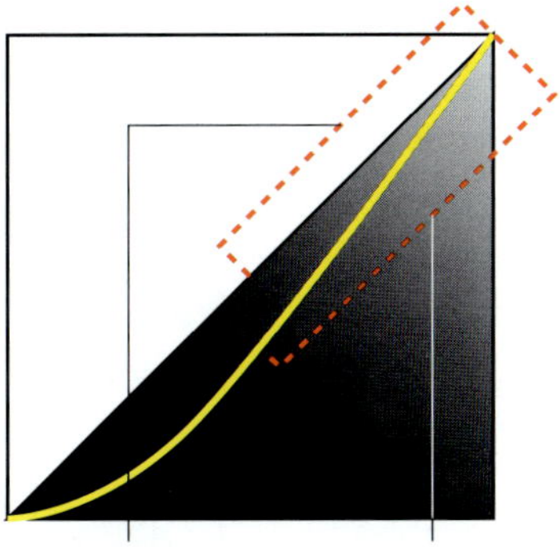

50 – 100% is displayed on the monitor using this number of greys

Adjusting the gamma distributes 50 – 100% amongst this many greys

Colour gamuts

Each colour space has a different colour gamut – the range of colours it encompasses – and since they are device-dependent they vary from device to device. This diagram shows RGB and CMYK gamuts in relation to the CIE colour space, the space which underpins all other colour models. It shows the widest of the four to be the Scanner RGB and the narrowest to be the Offset press CMYK.

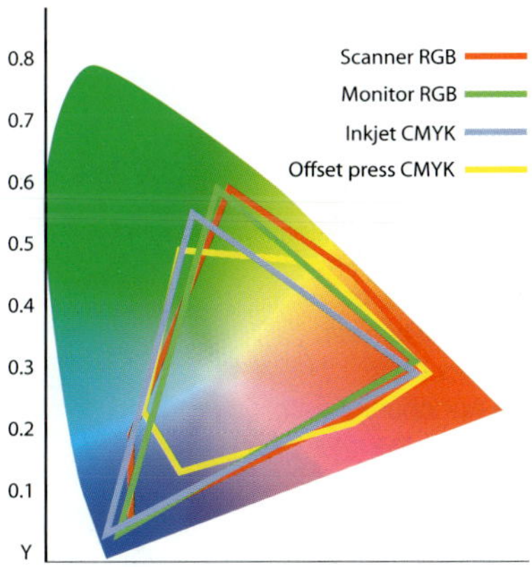

Simulated colours

Masks

Selection borders represent masks as animated lines (near right).

Such masks can be anti-aliased and feathered. In Quick Mask mode unselected areas are shown overlaid with an editable colour tint (far right).

Masks can be stored for later use in greyscale alpha channels (near right).

Editing work is restricted to unmasked areas (far right).

Anti-aliasing

Anti-aliasing softens – gradates – the edges of type and selections to give smoother, sharper-looking, edges. 11 pt type and below is best left aliased as their forms are not chunky enough to take the gradating effect. Feathering also involves gradation, the difference being that more pixels are modified to give an obvious vignetted effect.

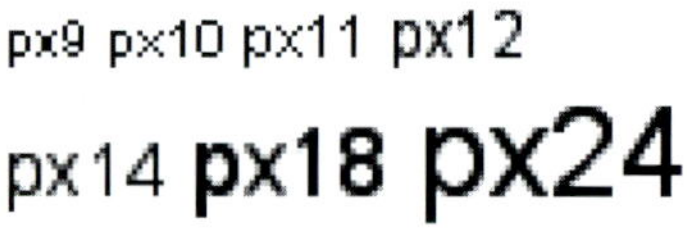

Examples of aliased 9, 10 and 11 pt/px type and anti-aliased 14, 18 and 24 pt type

Font (much enlarged) showing an anti-aliased character in green set against an aliased one in black

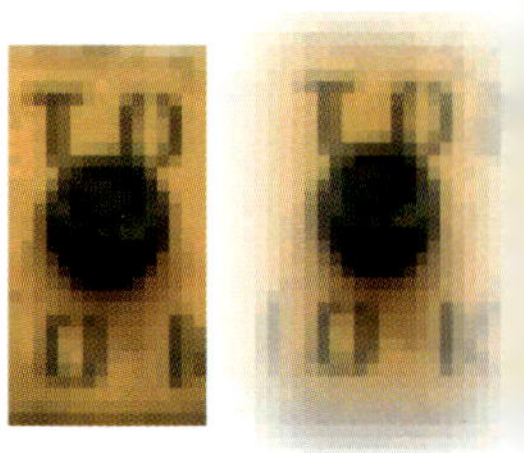

An image (much enlarged) with and without a 4 pt feathered edge

Adjust controls and filters

Tonal controls

Photoshop's Levels and Curves controls provide alternative means of altering the tonal levels.

You can adjust the tonal breadth of an image – its black and white points – in both controls. You can also adjust an image's brightness levels independently of its black and white points in either of them.

However, when it comes to adjusting contrast it's best to use Curves, as it can hold detail in highlight and shadow areas.

Bear in mind the following when adjusting tones.

- Most images benefit from having a black and a white somewhere.
- Increasing contrast gives a bit of 'zap' to an image but has the effect of reducing the number of tones and thus image detail.

Colour balance controls

Photoshop's Levels, Colour Balance and Variations controls provide alternative means of correcting colour casts.

It's probably best to restrict yourself to either the Levels or Colour Balance controls, if only because you can more easily see the effect of changes in the document window. In the Variations control you are restricted to miniature previews.

The interaction of colours

Colour rebalancing is perhaps the hardest type of adjustment to make, as it requires not only good colour perception but also an understanding of the way component colours interact with one other.

The RGB and CMYK diagram (see colour section) shows the relationship of component colours in a colour image. Notice that equal proportions of red and blue make magenta, equal proportions of blue and green make cyan and equal proportions of green and red make yellow.

Of course, the whole gamut of hues (all the colours in the rainbow) should really be shown in the diagram, from red, violet, indigo, blue, green, yellow, through to orange and back to red again.

Colour balance

Colour balance is best explained by referring to the colour balance diagram (see colour section) showing the three colour axes.

When colours are unbalanced, images will have a preponderance of a hue, such as red. To correct the imbalance you need to either adjust the axis of the problem colour, in this case the red:cyan axis, or one or more of the other axes. It depends which axis or axes are really at fault.

If an image looks too orange, the problem colour is somewhere between red and yellow on the colour wheel. In situations such as this adjustments will need to be made to at least two axes, in this case the red:cyan axis and the blue:yellow axis. By reducing the red in one and strengthening the blue in the other the image will be brought back into line.

Sometimes the Channels palette is a good guide to which colour is out of kilter. If one thumbnail is much lighter or darker than the rest, it probably represents the faulty channel. If it's very light, it means the colour is too strong; if it's very dark, it means it's too weak (see Figure 10.1).

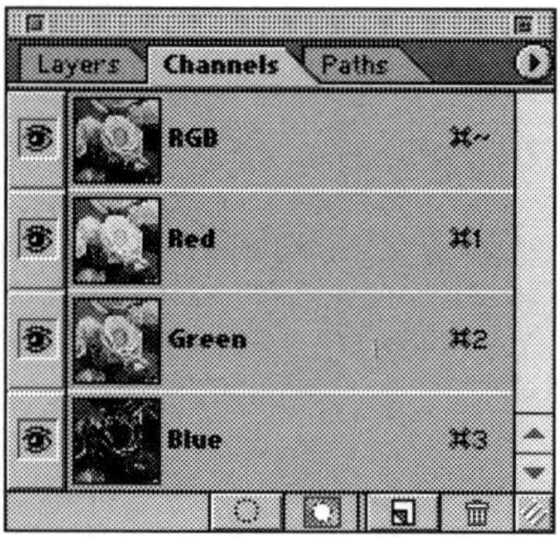

Figure 10.1 Dark-looking 'Blue' thumbnail suggests its channel is too weak

Skin colours are often difficult to get right. Pass the cursor over such areas and check the values in the Info palette. For a pale complexion in normal lighting conditions the figures for the magenta and yellow should be roughly equal and the figure for the cyan should be roughly half – e.g. c 19, m 42, y 39.

Bear in mind the following when balancing colours:

- Because of the interaction between opposing colours, only fine adjustments are usually necessary.
- Colours can be re-balanced by adjusting the problem colour(s) or adjusting opposing colour(s).
- Colour balancing affects the brightness (luminance) and saturation of images.
- You can limit colour balance to shadow, midtone or highlight areas in most controls.

Selective colour control

Photoshop's Selective control provides the means of removing unwanted constituent colours.

When colours appear impure they will contain too much of the opposing colour on the colour wheel. To purify the colour you need to reduce or remove this colour. For instance, a bright-red shirt should, in CMYK terms, have high magenta and yellow values and a low cyan value, particularly in its non-shadow areas. If the cyan is overstrong it will make the red appear dirty. In a situation such as this a selective adjustment needs to be made in the red passages of the image. By reducing the cyan all the reds in the image will be cleaned up.

Saturation controls

The saturation of an image determines the cleanliness of colours. When colours are low in saturation they are greyed. When colours are highly saturated, the opposite occurs; colours appear over-rich and artificial.

Drab-looking images can often benefit from a slight increase in saturation to inject a bit of life into them whilst perfectly good images may be heavily desaturated to give a subtle, colour-wash effect, thereby enhancing their dramatic appeal.

Photoshop's Variations and Hue/Saturation controls provide alternative means of altering saturation. Although both controls affect the image in the same way, try to use Hue/Saturation for your work if only because you can see the effect of changes more easily. You are not restricted to miniature previews.

When adjusting saturation bear the following in mind:

- Decreases in saturation have no negative effect on image quality.
- Even small increases in saturation can easily move colours outside the CMYK colour gamut.
- Large increases in saturation invariably make colours appear artificial.
- Increasing saturation does not necessarily add much colour to monochromatic images.

Enhancing filters

Photoshop's sharpening filters provide alternative means to improve image sharpness.

Both Sharpen and Sharpen More add detail to an image by increasing the contrast between adjacent pixels (the latter filter has a stronger effect than the former). Both tend to make images 'noisy' (spotty).

Sharpen Edges and Unsharp Mask on the other hand sharpen by increasing edge contrast within images, with no noise being added.

When choosing which filter to use bear the following in mind:

- Sharpen or Sharpen More filters should be used only if you wish to give 'grit' to an image.
- Unsharp Mask is the best general sharpening filter. It doesn't add noise and it's user-adjustable.

Preparing for correction work

Specifying colour settings

Photoshop's colour setting profiles control how images appear on screen and how they output in print. By default, the profiles are automatically embedded in documents.

① Choose Colour Settings… from the Edit menu. The Colour Settings dialog box will be displayed (See Figure 10.2).

② Choose either a pre-press or web graphics option from the Settings pop-up menu.

③ Under Working Spaces, choose a coated, uncoated or newsprint option from the CMYK pop-up menu. If the paper stock you plan to use is matt or gloss coated choose Coated. If you plan to use an uncoated stock, such as a cartridge or stationery paper, choose Uncoated.

④ Click OK.

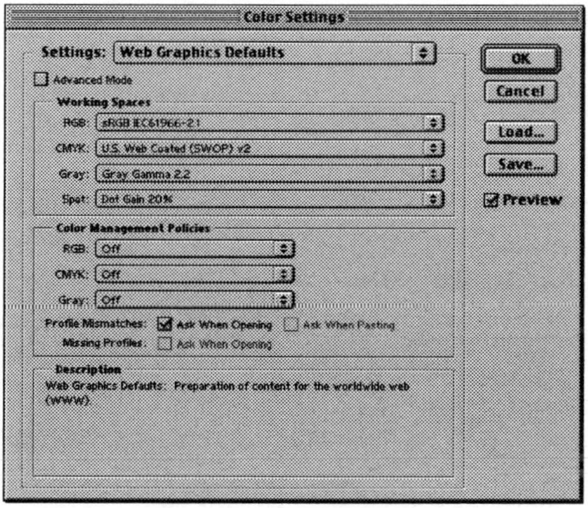

Figure 10.2 The Colour Settings dialog box

Checking pixel values

Display the Info palette at all times (Figure 10.3) so you can check the colour values of pixels within an image and see the effect of adjustments.

By default, RGB data is shown on the left with CMYK data on the right. The complementary colours line up. This is useful as it reminds you which RGB colour affects which CMY colour.

When you make adjustments in any of the controls, the Info palette displays before and after values.

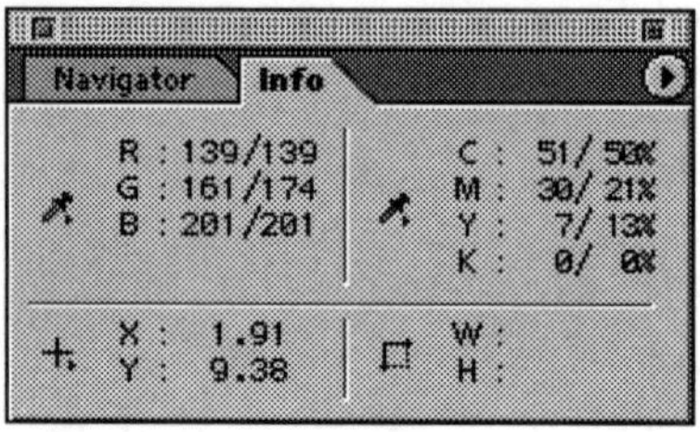

Figure 10.3 The Info palette showing before and after figures

① Choose Show Info from the Window menu.

② Move the cursor over the area of the image you wish to examine. The palette displays the RGB and CMYK (or greyscale) values of the pixels at the cursor location (see Figure 10.3).

▲ RGB colour values range from 0 to 255; CMYK values from 0 to 100%.

Preparing channel thumbnails

Display the Channel palette at all times so you can check the strength of image channels and see the effect of adjustments.

When you make adjustments in any of the Adjust controls, the thumbnails alter in relative brightness.

① Choose Display and Cursors… from the Preferences sub-menu in the Edit menu.

② Uncheck Colour Channels in Colour.

③ Click OK.

④ Choose Palette Options from the pop-up menu.

⑤ Select the largest thumbnail.

⑥ Click OK.

Undoing setting in dialog boxes

● Hold down Alt and click Reset if you wish to undo settings without closing a dialog box.

The correction regime

The correction regime can involve six different processes, with most involving a choice of settings.

- Setting black and white points.
- Adjusting brightness.
- Adjusting contrast.
- Balancing colours.
- Adjusting saturation.
- Sharpening.

Most images require the resetting of black and white points. Other adjustments need only be made if an image has further deficiencies.

When using the controls and filters bear the following in mind:

- Make adjustments in the order as listed and avoid applying the same process more than once. Over-correction leads to inevitable loss of tonal and colour detail.
- Access the Adjust controls through adjustment layers so that adjustments are reversible (see Chapter 13).
- Don't make adjustments for the sake of it unless you are practising; if an image looks OK, leave it alone, even though it may be incorrect from a purely technical point of view.
- Ensure your monitor is properly calibrated and that Photoshop's colour settings are correct before you make any corrections.

Improving tonal values

Most images should have a full range of tonal values, ranging from black in the shadow areas through to white in the highlight areas. In practice, images tend to lack blacks and whites and this needs to be rectified.

You can set the points automatically for average key images. Photoshop selects the darkest and lightest pixels in an image and adjusts them accordingly.

However, it's usually best to set the points yourself by either dragging the black and white input sliders or using the eyedroppers. The latter method enables you to set points at specific pixel locations. You may, for example, wish to make part of a pale cream shirt white and 'burn out' a whiter area representing the bright bodywork of a car.

Setting black and white points

Use the Levels control to set the black and white points and to adjust brightness levels.

① Choose Levels… from the Adjust sub-menu in the Image menu. The Levels dialog box will be displayed (see Figure 10.4).

② Either:

Click Auto. Use this method for average key (normal brightness) images only.

Or:

Move the left and/or right sliders of the Input levels inward to align with the ends of the histogram (see Figure 10.4).

Or:

Select the black eyedropper and click on the pixel in the image you wish to be black. Skip this step for high key (very bright) images.

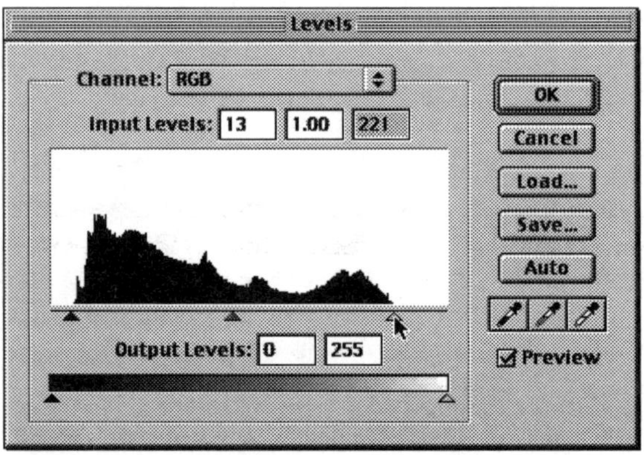

Figure 10.4 Setting an image's black and white points

③ Select the white eyedropper and click on the pixel you wish to be white. Skip this step for low key (very dark) images.

Adjusting brightness levels

Use the Levels control instead of Brightness/Contrast to adjust brightness, as it does not disturb previously set black and white point settings.

① Move the centre slider of the Input levels left to increase brightness or right to reduce brightness (see Figure 10.5).

② Click OK.

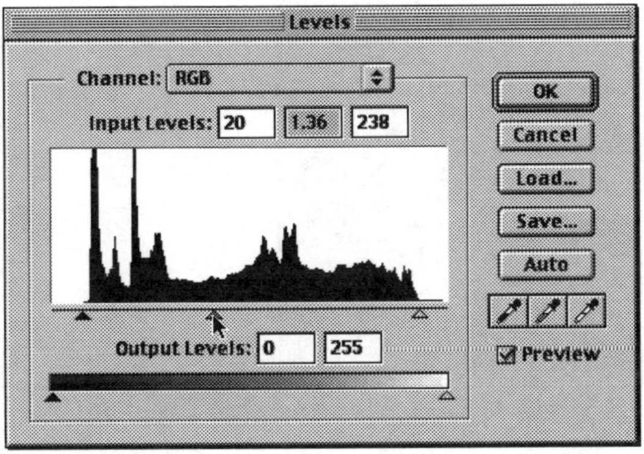

Figure 10.5 Adjusting the brightness – gamma – of an image whilst maintaining its blacks and whites

Increasing contrast

Use the Curves control rather than the Levels or Brightness/Contrast to adjust contrast as it can maintain detail in the shadow and highlight areas. Notice it has the same eyedroppers as the Levels control.

① Choose Curves… from the Adjust sub-menu in the Image menu. The Curves dialog box will be displayed (see Figure 10.6).

② Set the black and white points using the black and white eyedroppers as described earlier. Only do this if you have not already set the points in the Levels control.

③ Click twice on the diagonal line to add two anchor points.

④ Move the points to curve the line into a flattened ‘s’ shape (see Figure 10.6).

⑤ Click OK.

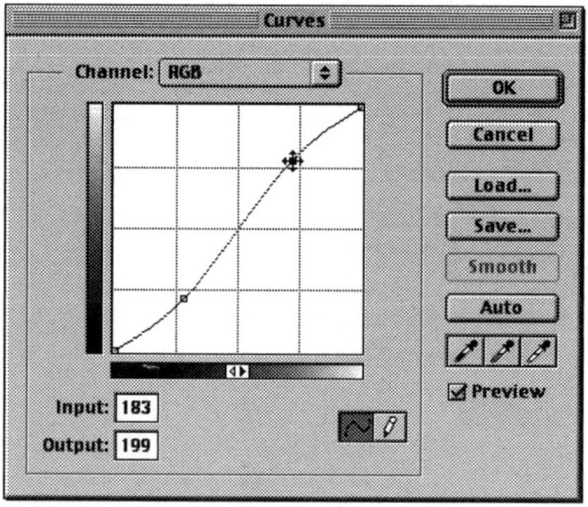

Figure 10.6 Creating an ‘s’ curve to increase the contrast of an image

Balancing colours

Whilst colour imbalance is often an image-wide problem, it is not always so. Sometimes its effect is more marked in some tonal levels than others. For instance, colours may look acceptable in the lighter passages of an image but not in the darker ones.

Colours may also look wrong if differently lit. Subjects illuminated partly by tungsten light and shot with daylight film will display localized colour casts.

In such cases, mask off areas which don’t require adjustment by using the selection tools.

Correcting colour casts

Use the Levels control to correct overall colour casts.

① Choose Levels... from the Adjust sub-menu in the Image menu. The Levels dialog box will be displayed.

② Select a colour from the Channel pop-up menu.

③ Move the centre slider of the Input levels left to increase the strength of the colour or right to reduce the strength of the colour (see Figure 10.7).

④ Click OK.

▲ To undo all settings, hold down the Alt key and press Reset.

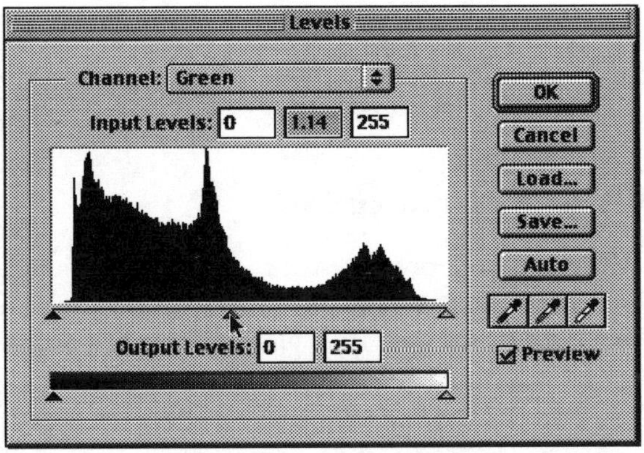

Figure 10.7 Increasing the green in the image

Alternatively, use the Colour Balance control to correct colour casts restricted to shadow, midtone or highlights areas. This control has an added feature: it preserves luminosity levels when you make adjustments.

① Choose Colour Balance... from the Adjust sub-menu in the Image menu. The Colour Balance dialog box will be displayed.

② Check Preserve Luminosity to maintain brightness levels.

③ Click Shadows, Midtones or Highlights.

④ Move the sliders away from a colour name to reduce it and towards a colour to strengthen it (see Figure 10.8).

⑤ Click OK.

✚ The values at the top of the box show the changing values of the red, green and blue channels respectively.

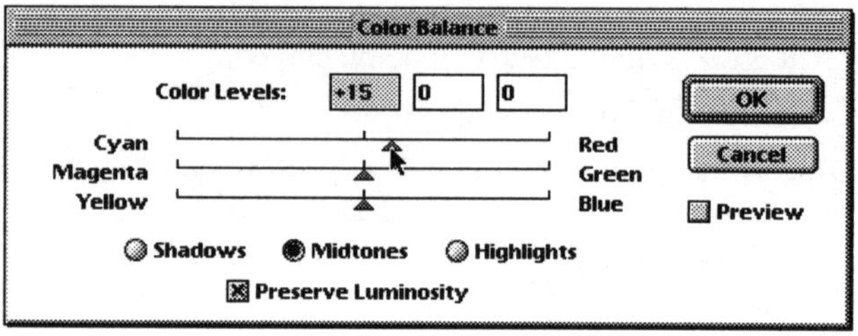

Figure 10.8 Reducing a magenta cast by increasing the green and reducing the red and blue channels

Balancing colours with visual options

You can also use the Variations control to correct colour casts. This control is good for first-timers as it has miniature previews to guide you. The downside is that it's not easy to see the effect of adjustments at such a small viewing scale.

① Choose Variations... from the Adjust sub-menu in the Image menu. The Variations dialog box will be displayed.

② Select Shadows, Midtones or Highlights.

③ Adjust the Fine/Coarse slider to set the degree of difference between the images surrounding the Current Pick in the bottom left panel of the dialog box.

④ Click on one of the six images surrounding the Current Pick in the bottom left panel to add more of a colour. Each time you click, the Current Pick will be updated in all three panels (see Figure 10.9).

⑤ Hold down [Alt] and click Reset if you wish to undo any changes without closing the dialog box.

⑥ Click OK.

✚ Check Show Clipping to identify images with shadow and highlight areas which will be converted to solid black or solid white if chosen.

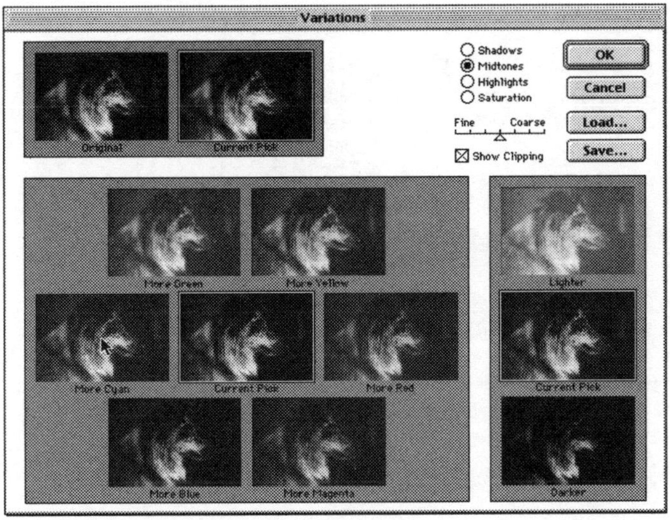

Figure 10.9 Increasing the cyan in an image

Balancing colours with grey subjects

If a neutral grey should present in the image, such as an area of metal or a grey hat, move the cursor over the pixels to check their values.

The Info palette should indicate practically equal values for red, green and blue. If the values are unequal, such as R: 155, G: 175, B: 135, an overall colour cast is present.

① Choose Levels… from the Adjust sub-menu in the Image menu. The Levels dialog box will be displayed.

② Select the middle (grey) eyedropper (see Figure 10.10).

③ Click on a pixel which you consider should be of a neutral value. The pixel values will be equalized to remove any traces of colour. All other pixels within the image will be adjusted on a relative basis.

④ Click OK.

▲ Close in on the greyer pixels in the image by pressing Command-Space.

The eyedropper should be set to Pantone Cool Grey 8 CV by double-clicking its icon and selecting the colour in the Custom Colours dialog box.

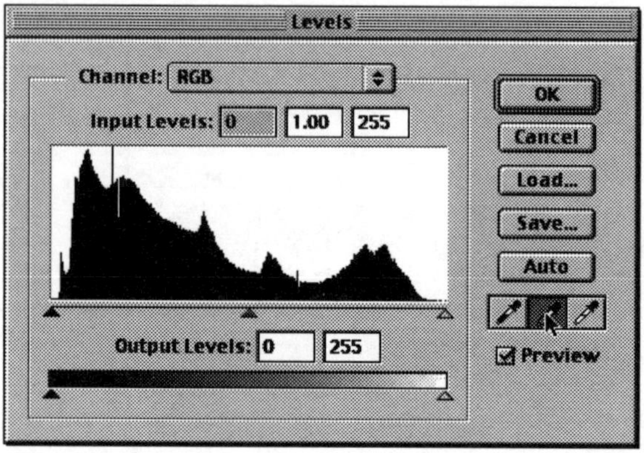

Figure 10.10 One way of removing a colour cast in an image

Adjusting saturation

Adjusting saturation levels

Use the Hue/Saturation control to adjust the overall saturation of an image.

① Choose Gamut Warning from the View menu. Oversaturated colours will appear grey within an image. This optional step is important for print images.

② Choose Hue/Saturation… from the Adjust sub-menu in the Image menu. The Hue/Saturation dialog box will be displayed.

③ Check Preview.

④ Moving the Saturation slider to the left reduces the saturation, to the right increases saturation (see Figure 10.11).

⑤ Click OK.

⑥ Choose Gamut Warning from the View menu to untick the command.

▲ You can also view how an image will look in CMYK. Choose Working CMYK from the Proof Setup sub-menu in the View menu to tick the command. CMYK will appear in parentheses after RGB in the title bar of the document window. Remember to untick the command to return to the RGB screen rendition.

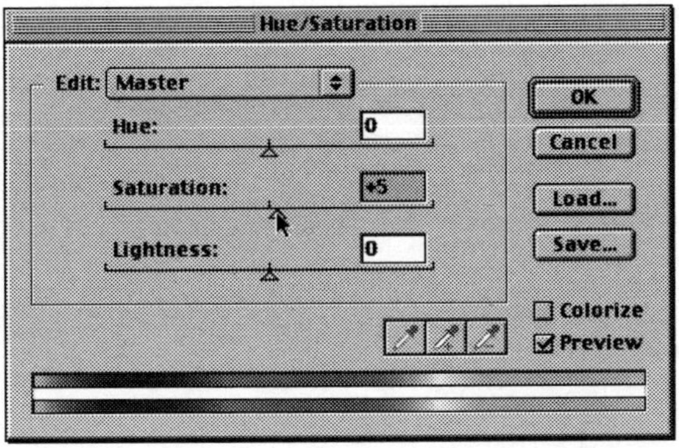

Figure 10.11 Increasing the saturation of an image

Adjusting saturation using visual options

① Choose Variations… from the Adjust sub-menu in the Image menu. The Variations dialog box will be displayed (see Figure 10.12).

② Select Saturation.

③ Adjust the Fine/Coarse slider to set the degree of difference between the images surrounding the Current Pick in the bottom left panel of the dialog box.

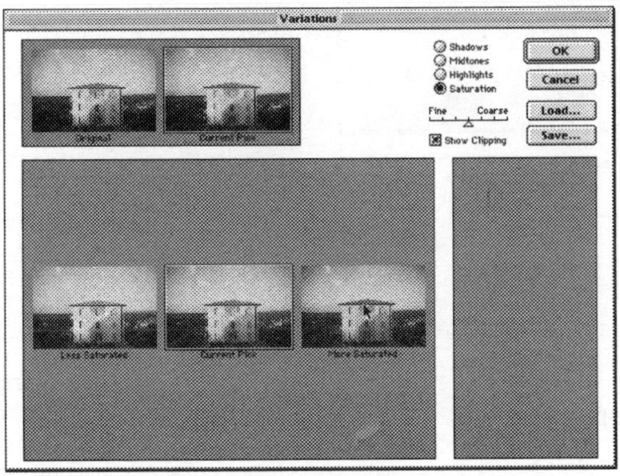

Figure 10.12 Increasing saturation in an image

④ Click on one of the images on either side of the Current Pick in the bottom left panel to alter the saturation. Each time you click, the Current Pick will be updated in both panels.

⑤ Click OK.

▲ Check Show Clipping to identify images with areas that will become over-saturated if chosen.

Cleaning up colours

Removing unwanted colours

① Choose Selective Colour… from the Adjust sub-menu in the Image menu. The Selective Colour dialog box will be displayed (see Figure 10.13).

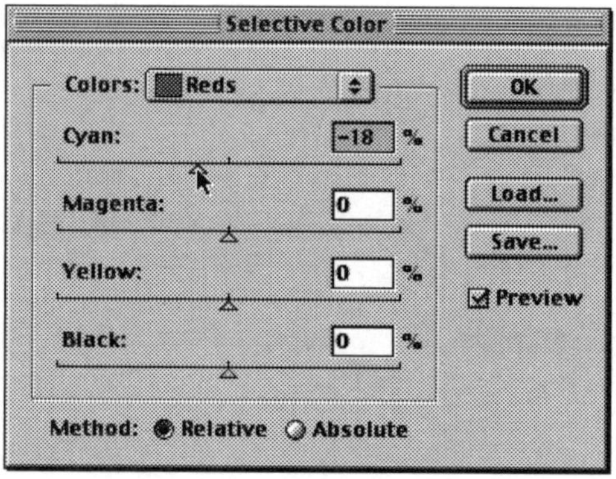

Figure 10.13 Removing an unwanted colour

② Check Preview.

③ Choose a target colour from the Colours pop-up menu.

④ Select Relative if you do not wish adjustments to affect highlight areas.

⑤ Move the appropriate slider to the left to reduce the strength of the component colour.

⑥ Click OK.

Improving image definition

Applying Sharpen and Sharpen More

Use these filters for improving the focus of blurred subjects or for refocusing images that have become blurred through extreme resampling.

- Choose Sharpen or Sharpen More from the Sharpen sub-menu in the Filter menu.

Applying Unsharp Mask

Use the filter for general sharpening work. Print images should be slightly oversharpened to compensate for the softening effect of halftone screens. Edges should display distinct 'haloing' on screen when viewed at a scale roughly one and a half times print size. Because sharpening limits the usefulness of images it's best applied to production copies rather than to masters.

Screen images should look sharp but not oversharp – what you see really is what you get – so view them at 100% scale (actual pixels) to get the sharpness absolutely right. They should, of course, be at a resolution of 72 ppi before any sharpening takes place.

① Choose Unsharp Mask… from the Sharpen sub-menu in the Filter menu. The Unsharp Mask dialog box will be displayed (see Figure 10.14).

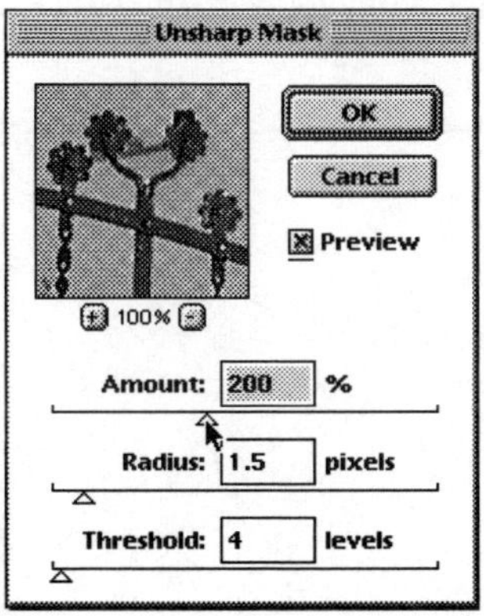

Figure 10.14 Increasing the sharpness of an image

② Click on an area of the image in the document window. The area will automatically show in the dialog box window.

③ Click the + or – signs to enlarge or reduce the preview image.

④ Set the Radius to 1/200th of the image resolution (for example, 1.0 for a 200 ppi image), the Threshold to 3 or 4 and the Amount (degree of sharpness) to an appropriate figure, usually somewhere between 100 and 150% (see Figure 10.14).

⑤ Press the preview image to view the original state of the image. Alternatively, uncheck Preview to view the original state of the image in the document window.

⑥ Click OK.

Summary

Image problems tend to be related to tone, colour or sharpness.

Up to six different processes can be involved in image correction.

Tonal values are enhanced by setting the black and white points, and by adjusting gamma and contrast levels.

Colour balance is achieved by strengthening or weakening one or more constituent colours.

Unwanted colours in images can be reduced or removed by using Selective colour.

Unsharp Mask is the best filter for improving edge sharpness.

11 DRAWING AND EDITING SHAPES

You can create graphic shapes for logo elements, navigation buttons and such like using Photoshop's vector drawing tools. You do this by working in shape layers. You can also create paths – shapes without colour fills – for conversion into selection borders or for specifying as clipping paths.

Unlike pixels, vector shapes are discrete graphic objects. They can be selected, moved and reshaped without affecting other objects and without leaving traces of changes. Since they are also resolution-independent, they maintain their crisp edges when resized.

Creating shapes and work paths

Creating shapes

① Choose a foreground colour. The colour will be used for the shapes.

② Choose Show Layers… from the Window menu. The Layers palette will be displayed.

③ Select the pen tool or one of the shape tools.

④ Select the Create New Shape Layer button in the Options bar (see Figure 11.1).

Figure 11.1 Pen tool options showing New Shape Layer button

⑤ Create a shape with the selected tool. A new Shape layer with linked Layer clipping path will appear in the Layers palette.

⑥ To create further shapes on the same layer, continue drawing shapes (see Figure 11.2).

⑦ Choose a shape area option to specify how the shapes behave when they overlap.

⑧ Press to dismiss the drawing tools.

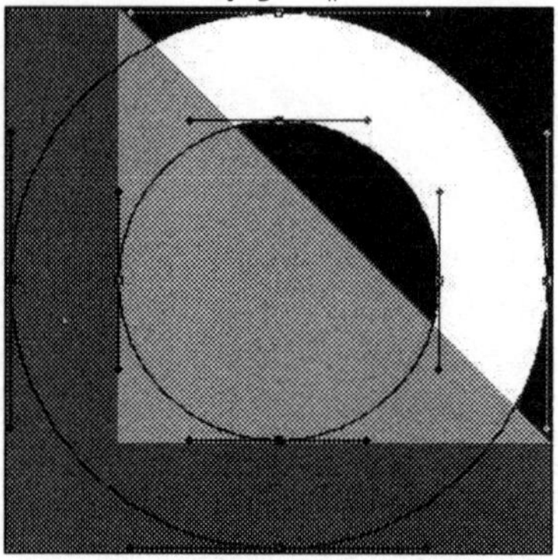

Figure 11.2 Shapes drawn with the Pen and Ellipse tools

▲ To add shapes to an existing Shape layer, first select the Shape layer and then start drawing.

Saving custom shapes

① Select a shape layer in the Layers palette or a path in the Paths palette.

② Choose Define Custom Shape from the Edit menu. The Shape name dialog box will be displayed.

③ Name the shape and press . The custom shape will automatically be listed in the Custom Shapes pop-up menu in the Options bar.

Creating work paths

You use work paths primarily to create cut-outs. Do this by drawing around the perimeter of an image, such as around the edge of a coffee pot.

If you convert the resulting path into a selection border and then inverse it, you can fill outlying areas with a colour of your choice. Alternatively, if you specify it to be a clipping path, you can mask off the outlying areas, effectively making them transparent (this incidentally is the only way to create transparency in printed halftones).

To create cut-outs for screen display, it's necessary to give images a white background. You can then use the Ink Effect controls within authoring programs or the transparency controls within certain web file conversion programs to specify the white areas to be transparent.

To create cut-outs for the web, it's necessary to give images a transparent background. This is achieved by working on layers and deleting areas to transparent.

① Choose Show Paths… from the Window menu. The Paths palette will be displayed.

② Select the pen tool.

③ In the Options bar, select the Create New Work Path button.

④ Click or click-drag the pen to create a closed path around the perimeter of a subject, such as the shape of person. A new Work Path will appear in the Paths palette (see Figure 11.3).

⑤ To create multiple paths, continue drawing closed paths.

✚ You can draw a path within a path if you wish to create transparent areas within cut-outs.

Saving a work path

① Choose Save Path… from the Paths palette menu. The New Path dialog box will be displayed.

② Name the path, such as 'cut-out'.

③ Click OK. The name will appear in the Paths palette (see Figure 11.3).

Figure 11.3 The Paths palette

! When a saved path is selected in the Paths palette it is not protected from deletion.

Creating a selection border from a work path

Once you've created a path, you can convert it into a selection border.

① Create a path.

② Press [Alt] and click the Make Selection button in the Paths palette (see Figure 11.4). The Make Selection dialog box will be displayed (see Figure 11.5).

③ Check Anti-aliased.

④ Enter a value in the Feather field.

⑤ Click OK.

⑥ Click the blank area beneath path name(s) in the palette to turn off path.

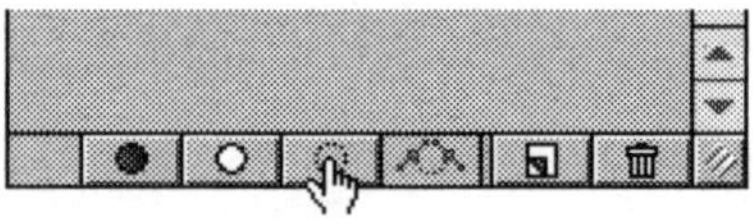

Figure 11.4 Creating a selection border from a work path

▲ As an alternative to using work paths as a basis for creating selection borders, you can create rasterized shapes on layers using the shape tools. Instead of selecting Create New Shape layer, select Create Filled Region and specify a blending mode, layer opacity and aliasing option. Then use the shape tools in the normal manner.

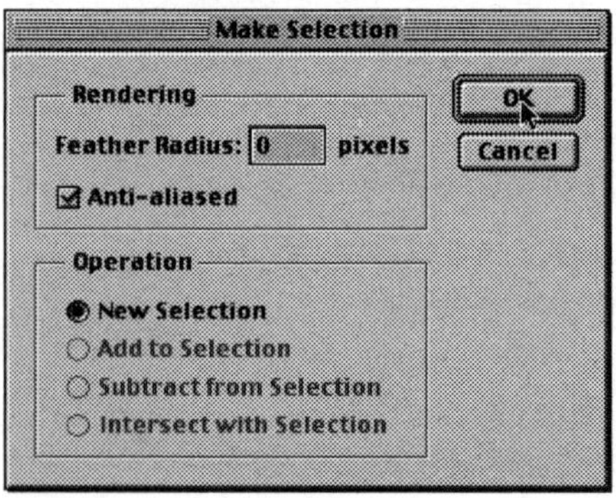

Figure 11.5 The Make Selection dialog box

Creating a work path from a selection border

You can convert a selection border into a work path although Photoshop does not always do it that successfully.

① Create a selection border using one of the selection tools.

② Press [Alt] and click the Make Work Path button in the Paths palette (see Figure 11.6). The Make Work Path dialog box will be displayed (see Figure 11.7).

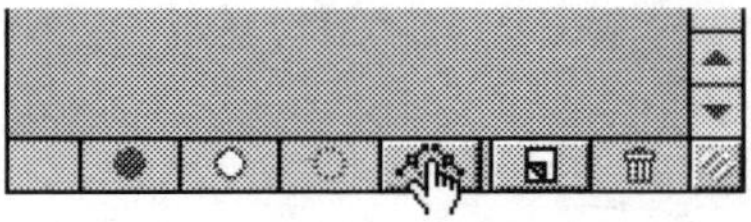

Figure 11.6 Creating a work path from a selection border

③ Enter a value in the Tolerance field (the lower the figure the closer the path will follow the edge of the selection). The new work path will be added to the Paths palette.

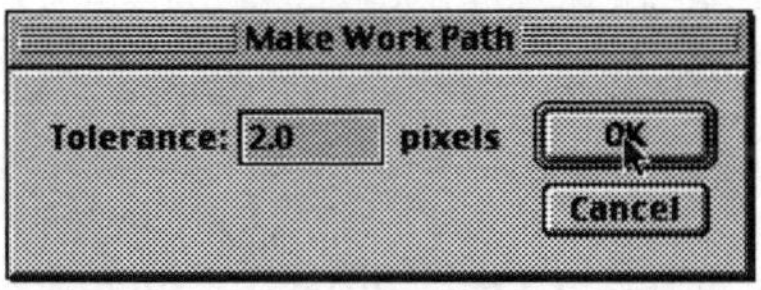

Figure 11.7 The Make Work Path dialog box

Specifying a clipping path

For paths to act as transparency masks in printed greyscale and colour images it's necessary to specify them as clipping paths (see Figure 11.8).

Figure 11.8 Image without a clipping path and with a clipping path

① Create and save a path.

② Choose Clipping path from the Paths palette menu. The Clipping Path dialog box will be displayed (see Figure 11.9).

③ Choose the saved path from the Path pop-up menu. Enter 1 in the Flatness field.

④ Click OK.

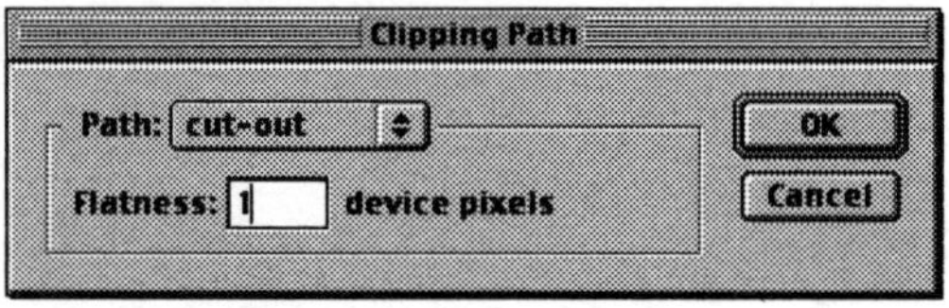

Figure 11.9 Clipping Path dialog box

▲ You can specify white areas to be transparent in line (bitmap) images, provided they are saved in EPS format.

! Save a document with a clipping path in EPS format for QuarkXPress version 3 or later and TIFF format for Adobe PageMaker version 6 or later.

Saving images with clipping paths

Images with clipping paths need to be saved in TIFF format for inclusion in PageMaker documents and EPS format for inclusion in QuarkXPress documents. (See Chapter 13.)

Turning off a path

- Click blank area beneath path name(s) in the Paths palette.

Turning on a path

- Click on path name in the Paths palette.

! When a path is saved and on (selected) it is not protected from deletion.

Using the shape tools

You can create simple geometric shapes within Photoshop without having to draw them from scratch (see Figure 11.2). And because the resulting paths are editable you can use them as a starting point for more complex forms.

Whether you are good at drawing or not, use the tools to create the shapes as you can be sure of their accurate construction.

There are five standard shape tools and an option for creating your own custom tools.

Setting shape tool options

Each shape tool provides specific options.

The rectangle, rounded rectangle and ellipse have the following settings: unconstrained, square (circle), fixed size: w_ h_ or proportional: w_ h_ ; from centre and snap to pixels.

The polygon has the following settings: radius…, smooth corners, indent sides by_ and smooth indents.

Arrow heads: start, end, width_, length_ and concavity_.

Using the shape tools

When click-dragging:

- Hold down Shift to constrain a rectangle or rounded-rectangle into a square, an ellipse into a circle and a line angle to a multiple of 45 degrees.
- Hold down Option to draw from the centre of a shape.
- Hold down Space to move a shape.

Drawing with the Pen tool

The Pen tool (see Figure 11.10) allows you to create straight lines and curves with utmost precision. It's the most flexible and powerful of the tools and with it you can create any shape you desire.

Figure 11.10 The Pen tool

You draw with the Pen tool by clicking or click-dragging with the mouse. Clicking the mouse creates corner points and click-dragging creates smooth points, complete with direction lines (see Figure 11.11).

Figure 11.11 Clicking creates straight line segments (left) whilst click-dragging creates curved segments (right). Fills excluded and segments selected for clarity

Drawing straight lines

① With the Pen tool selected, position the tip of the pen cursor where you wish the straight line to begin. (A small multiplication sign will appear beside the pen cursor to denote it's ready to create the first point.) Click to create the first anchor point. The anchor point remains selected (appears solid) until the next point is created.

② Click again where you wish the first straight line segment to end.

③ Click again at the end of each straight line segment.

Completing paths

Use this method to close a path. Curved paths should be closed, otherwise a straight edge will be created between the two end points.

- Click the starting anchor point. (A small circle will appear beside the pen cursor to denote it's over the first point.)

Use this method to complete an open-ended path so you can start a new path:

- Press ⌘ and click on blank area of shape layer.

Redoing an anchor point

If you have made a mistake when creating an anchor point you can rectify the situation by one of the following actions.

Either:

- Choose Undo… from the Edit menu and then create a new anchor point.

Or:

- Press [Delete], click or click-drag the previous anchor point depending on whether it is a corner point or a smooth point. Then create a new anchor point.

Drawing curves

Drawing undulating curves

① With the Pen tool selected, position the tip of the pen cursor where you wish the wavy line to begin. (A small multiplication sign will appear beside the pen cursor to denote it's ready to create the first point.) Click-drag in a forward direction (tangentially to the first curve) to create the first anchor point. The anchor point remains selected (appears solid) until the next point is created.

② Click-drag again in the same manner at a position where you wish the curve to change direction.

③ Repeat step 2 for each change of curve direction (see Figure 11.12).

Figure 11.12 Smooth points where curves change direction. Fill excluded and segments selected for clarity

▲ When you create a smooth point adjust the length and orientation of its leading direction handle (the one the Pen tool is pulling out of the point) to create a trailing segment of the desired curvature. If this leading direction line is to be left in place (in the context of wavy lines it will be) it may need to be shortened if the following curved segment is short, otherwise the segment will be 'cockled'.

Curving in or out of a straight line

By aligning the direction lines of a smooth point with a trailing straight line segment a smooth transition is ensured between the two segments (see Figure 11.13).

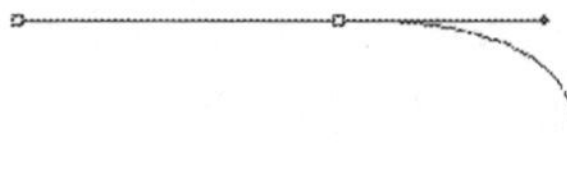

Figure 11.13 Aligning direction lines with a trailing straight line segment. Fill excluded and segments selected for clarity

Curving in and out of an angle

You draw curved segments from angles either by deleting the leading direction line of a smooth point or by adjusting its angle. Either way you need to select the Direct-selection tool before using the Pen tool.

By deleting the leading direction line of a smooth point, you can spring a new curved segment from the point.

① Click on the smooth point you have just created. (A small carat will appear beside the pen cursor to denote it's over the point.) Its leading direction line will be deleted (see Figure 11.14).

② Click-drag to create the next smooth point.

Figure 11.14 Newly created smooth point with two direction lines (left) and with its leading direction line removed and the next smooth point plotted (right). Fill excluded and segments selected for clarity

Rather than deleting the leading direction line you can adjust its angle to create a new curved segment of greater subtlety. At the same time as doing this you can also re-angle the trailing direction line to adjust the curve of the previous segment (see Figure 11.15).

① Hold down ⌘ and then Option once you have created a smooth point.

② Click-drag either direction point (the end point of either direction line).

Figure 11.15 Newly created smooth point with two direction lines (left) and with its leading direction line re-angled and the next smooth point plotted (right). Fills excluded and segments selected for clarity

Curving abruptly out of a straight line

By adding a leading direction to a corner point, you can spring a curved segment out from the point.

① Hold down Alt Option and click-drag from the corner point you have just created. (A small carat will appear beside the pen cursor to denote it's over the point.) A direction line will be drawn out of the point (see Figure 11.16). Orient the direction line to suit the curved segment yet to be drawn.

② Click-drag to create the next smooth point.

! The first direction line you add to a corner point will always be leading (controlling the following segment). The second direction line will be trailing (controlling the previous segment).

Figure 11.16 Corner point at end of straight segment (left) and with leading direction line added and the next smooth point plotted (right). Fills excluded and segments selected for clarity

Constraining points and direction lines

You can constrain direction lines and path angles to 45 degree increments.

Constraining anchor points

- Hold down Shift and click when creating corner points.

Constraining direction lines

- Hold down Shift and click-drag when creating smooth points.

Where to locate anchor points

The key to drawing with the tool is to know where to create points and how to configure their direction lines.

- Locate corner points:

  Where straight segments meet at a corner.

  Where curved segments spring out of straight segments.

  Where straight segments flow into curved segments.

  Where curved segments spring off in different directions.

- Locate smooth points:

  Where curved segments change direction.

  At the peaks and troughs of curves. The need for points at such locations depends on the complexity of the curve to be drawn.

Editing paths

Pen tool variants

There are three pen tool variants for path editing: Add-anchor-point, Delete-anchor-point and Convert-anchor-point (see Figure 11.17).

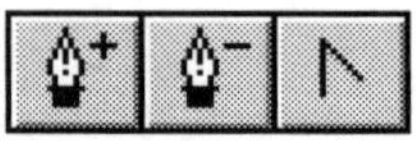

Figure 11.17 The Add-anchor-point, Delete-anchor-point and Convert-anchor-point tools

Adding, deleting and converting points

Adding a point

Either:

- With either the Pen or Add-anchor-point tool active, click on path segment. (A small plus sign will appear beside the pen cursor to denote it's over a segment.)

  Or:

- Select Add Anchor Points tool in the Toolbox.

  Anchor points will be added midway between existing points.

Deleting a point

● With either the Pen or Remove-anchor-point tool active, click on point. (A small minus sign will appear beside the pen cursor to denote it's over a point.)

▲ With the Remove-anchor-point tool active, hold down the Alt key to switch to the Add-anchor-point tool.

! Press Shift to override the add or remove capabilities of the Pen tool.

Converting a corner point to a smooth point

● With the Convert-direction-point tool active, click-drag from corner point. The leading direction line will always be the first to emerge.

▲ With the Pen tool active, hold down the Alt key to access this tool.

Converting a smooth point to a corner point

● With the Convert-direction-point tool active, click on point.

▲ With the Pen tool active, hold down the Alt key to access this tool.

Extending a path

① With the Pen tool active, click on end point. (A small forward slash will appear beside the pen cursor to denote it's over an end point.)

② Click or click-drag to extend path.

▲ The crossed-slash sign on the Pen tool cursor loses its rearward slash, indicating that the Pen tool is positioned over the end point.

Joining end points of two paths

● With the Pen tool active, click on each end point in turn.

Adjusting the line of a path

Moving a point

● With the Direct-direction tool active, click-drag point.

Moving a straight segment

- With the Direct-direction tool active, click-drag segment.

Adjusting a curve segment

With the Direct-direction tool active

Either:

- Click-drag segment.

Or:

- Select segment or associated point and click-drag end of direction handle.

Saving custom shapes

① Select a shape layer in the Layers palette or a path in the Paths palette.

② Choose Define Custom Shape… from the Edit menu. The Shape Name dialog box will be displayed.

③ Name the shape and click . The custom shape will automatically be listed in the Custom shapes pop-up menu in the Options bar.

Summary

When you select the Pen tool you have the choice of creating either a Shape layer or a work path.

Shape layers allow you to create vector shapes with coloured fills.

They are useful for drawing simple shapes for web buttons and suchlike.

Work paths drawn around shapes in an image can be converted to selection borders or specified as clipping paths.

Clipping paths are essential for masking off areas you wish to be transparent in images destined for print.

12 ADDING TYPE

Photoshop's latest type controls allow you add sophisticated typography to images and image composites. The controls are a boon for those working on web sites as pages can now incorporate rasterized – non-HTML – type to DTP standards.

Many of the controls are borrowed from Photoshop's sister program Illustrator so those of you already conversant with this program will feel immediately at home with them. For others the controls won't take long to master as they are very well thought out and easy to use.

Adding type

Type can be added to an image in one of two ways.

You can create either lines of type (called point type) or columns of type (called paragraph type). Either way a new type layer is added to the Layer palette and type is shown as bitmapped at the resolution of the image.

A variant of the Type tool allows you to set type vertically – characters stacked on top of each other – instead of lining up in a row.

But, whatever its configuration, type is edited in much the same way as in a word-processing document.

Creating point type

Short pieces of text, such as headings and captions, are achieved by creating point type. Such type doesn't self-wrap so the use of returns or shift-returns is essential for multi-lined texts.

Type created this way is often aligned with ruler guides or grids for accurate positioning.

① With the Type tool active, select Create a New Text Layer icon in the Options bar and click either Horizontal Orient Text or Vertical Orient Text.

② Type in text using the keyboard (see Figure 12.1). A new Text layer will be created (see page 134).

③ Press or click the Commit button in the Type tool Options bar to commit any changes.

Figure 12.1 A single line of point type

Creating paragraph type

Columns of type are achieved by creating paragraph type. The lines of type contained within the bounding box automatically wrap when they reach their edges.

Like point type, paragraph type is often aligned with ruler guides or grids.

① With the Type tool active, select the Create a New Text Layer icon in the Options bar and click either Horizontal Orient Text or Vertical Orient Text.

② Click-drag diagonally on artboard to define the column area. A paragraph type bounding box will be created on a new Text layer.

③ Type in text using the keyboard (see Figure 12.2). A new Text layer will be created (see page 134).

If you are unable to see any or all of the text enlarge the bounding box.

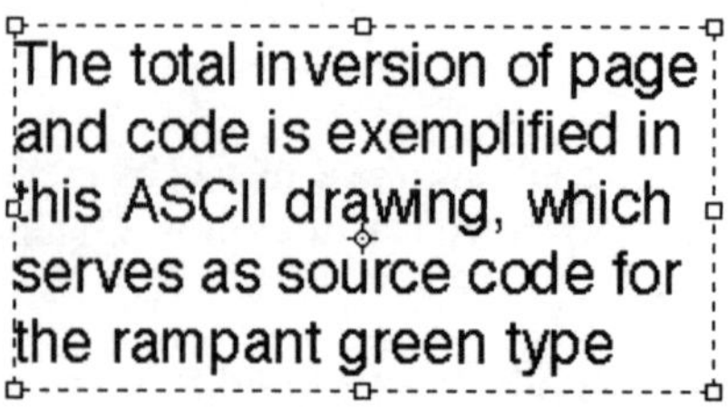

Figure 12.2 Paragraph type within its bounding box

④ Press or click the Commit button in the Type tool Options bar to commit any changes.

▲ Use the Vertical Type tool to create vertical lines of stacked characters.

Resizing bounding boxes

① With the Type tool active, click once somewhere within the bounding box (if it is not already selected) and move the pointer to one of its handles. Don't press the mouse button when you do this.

② The pointer turns into a double-arrow. Click-drag the handle to resize the bounding box (see Figure 12.3).

▲ Handles halfway along the side of the bounding boxes can be used to enlarge or reduce their width or height. Corner handles enable you to alter both dimensions at once.

Figure 12.3 Resizing a bounding box

Seeing all text in a column

If paragraph type overfills its bounding box, a small plus sign appears in the bottom right handle indicating that not all text is visible (see Figure 12.4). It's good practice to make adjustments to remove the sign even if the hidden text just comprises paragraph returns.

● Deepen or widen the bounding box.

Or: shorten the text.

Or: alter the type attributes.

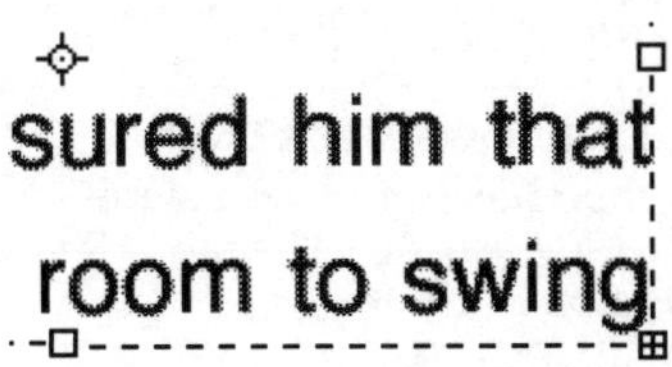

Figure 12.4 The presence of the plus sign in the bottom right handle of a bounding box indicates that there is more text to be displayed

Basic text editing

You edit text within Photoshop in much the same way as you do in most word-processing programs. You select the text and then add or delete text using the keyboard and copy or move text using the clipboard.

Selecting and submitting text

Text needs to be selected before any editing and formatting work can take place. Text is selected by using one of the type tools (see Figure 12.5). When a type tool is active, the dotted rectangle framing the I-beam cursor disappears when positioned over text.

Once editing and formatting work has been completed it's necessary to commit the text (effectively deselecting it) so you can move on.

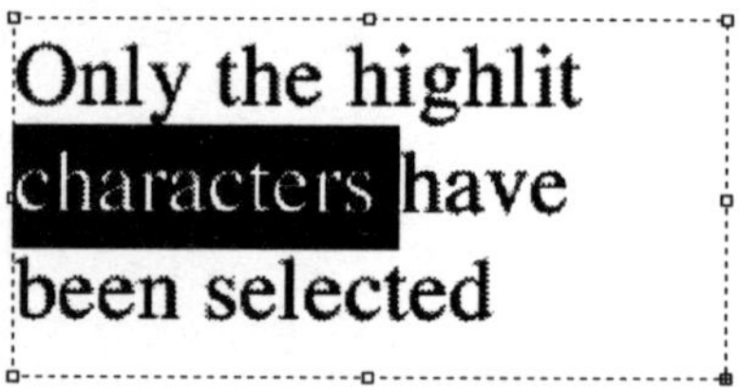

Figure 12.5 Characters selected by one of the type tools

Selecting text using one of the type tools

	Text to be selected	Number of clicks
●	Any contiguous text	Click-drag over text
●	Whole word (with space after)	Click twice on word
●	Whole paragraph	Click three times within paragraph
●	All text	Double-click text layer thumbnail in Layer palette

Selected characters in text are highlighted in colour.

▲ When selecting text by clicking, click to a regular beat and keep the body of the mouse steady.

Committing edits

- Press ↵ or click the Commit button in the Type tool Options bar to commit any changes (see Figure 12.6).

Cancelling edits

- Press ↵ or click the Cancel button in the Type tool Options bar to cancel any changes.

Figure 12.6 Type tool options showing the Commit and Cancel buttons on its far right

Deleting text

Either:

- Select the text and press Delete (back space).

Or:

- Position the insertion point to one side of the text to be deleted and press either Delete (back space) or Del.

Adding in extra text

① Position the insertion point where you wish to add text (make sure it's 'blinking' within the line of text or container).

② Type in the additional text.

Deleting text layers

- Select the Type layer in the Layers palette and click on the Wastebasket icon.

Basic formatting

Text needs to be given basic formatting, including such attributes as font, size, leading and alignment.

The first two attributes can be applied within the Type menu or by using the Character palette. Leading can only be applied within the Character palette and alignment within the Paragraph palette.

Applying essential attributes

① Click Palettes in the Options bar. The Character and Paragraph palettes will be displayed.

② Select the text to be styled using one of the methods described under Selecting text (page 126).

③ Choose a font from the Font, typestyle and size from their respective pop-up menus in the Options bar (see Figure 12.7). Alternatively, specify these attributes in the Character palette.

Figure 12.7 Type tool options

④ Choose a font colour by clicking on the Colour swatch in the Options bar.

⑤ Choose None, Crisp, Strong or Smooth from the Anti-aliasing method pop-up menu in the Options bar (see colour section).

⑥ Choose a value from the Leading pop-up menu in the Character palette. For normal text sizes (9–11 pt), the leading is usually 1–2 pt greater than the font size.

⑦ Choose from one of three alignments in the Options bar.

▲ Since the Character and Paragraph palettes are often used in sequence, nest them together to save time (see Chapter 2).

Formatting paragraphs

Formatting can be applied at a character or paragraph level within Photoshop. Character attributes can apply to any contiguous text, whether it's all the text on a layer or just a single character, whilst paragraph attributes always apply to whole paragraphs or multiples of paragraphs (see Figure 12.8).

As in most DTP and word-processing programs, paragraphs in Photoshop are defined by paragraph returns. These returns separate one paragraph from another and are entered using the Return key.

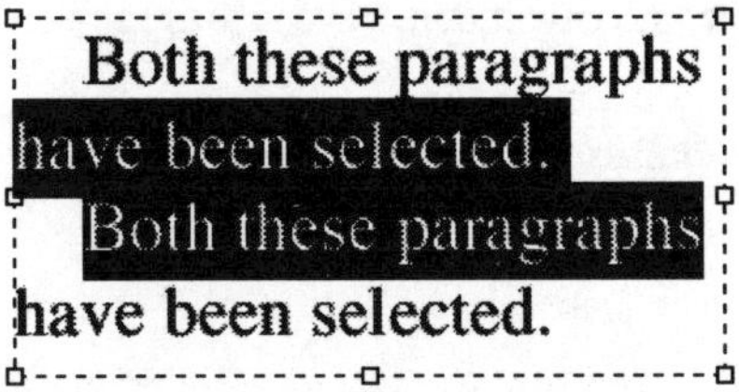

Figure 12.8 Paragraphs do not have to be fully selected for paragraph attributes to be applied

Indenting paragraphs

First-line indents are conventionally used to identify paragraph starts.

To create hanging indents for listing work, enter a positive value in the Left Indent field (such as 20 pt) and a negative value in First Line Left Indent field (such as –20 pt) (see Figure 12.9).

① Select a paragraph or paragraphs using one of the methods previously described.

② Click Palettes in the Options bar menu. The Paragraph palette will be displayed (see Figure 12.9).

③ Enter values in the indent fields. You can do this either by clicking one of the small triangles or by typing in a value.

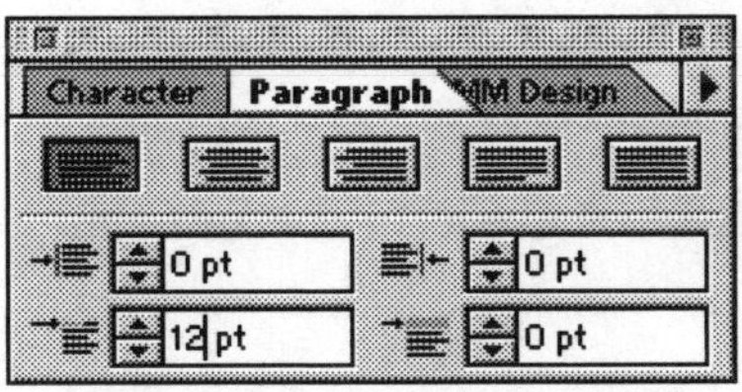

Figure 12.9 Setting a first-line indent

Inserting spaces before paragraphs

Use inter-paragraph spacing to reduce typographic density and to create visual pauses between paragraphs.

Inserting paragraph spaces

① Select a paragraph or paragraphs using one of the methods previously described.

② Click Palettes in the Options bar menu. The Paragraph palette will be displayed.

③ Enter a value in the Space Before field. You can do this by clicking the small triangles or by typing (see Figure 12.10).

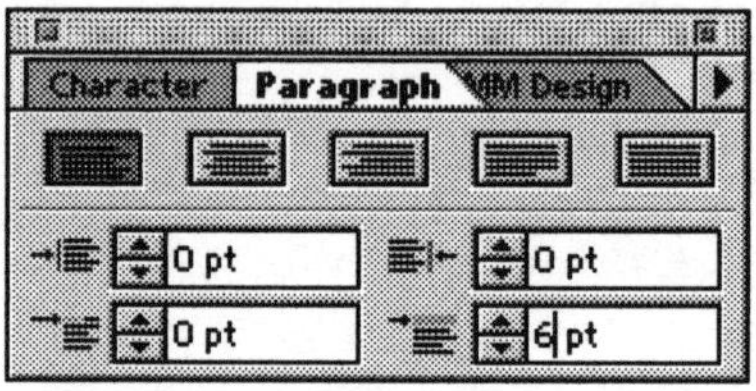

Figure 12.10 Inserting a space before a paragraph

Spacing words

You can alter the tracking of text for reasons of design, copyfitting or legibility (see Figure 12.11). Tracking is measured 1/1000th of an em space (an em space being roughly the width of a capital M). Untracked word and character spaces are set at 0.

Figure 12.11 Text being negatively 'tracked' for visual effect

① Select the text to be tracked using one of the methods previously described.

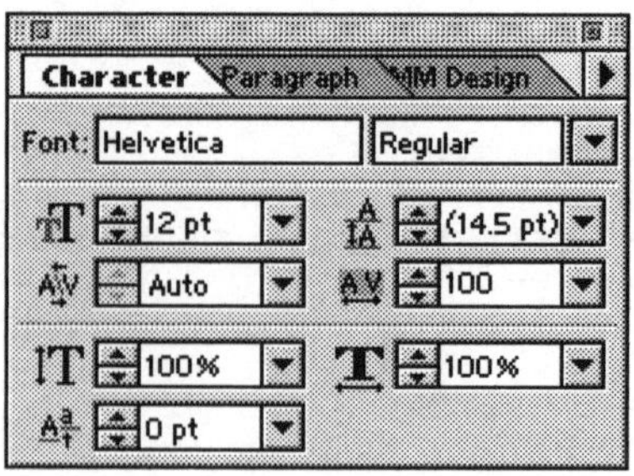

Figure 12.12 Tracking characters by 100/1000 em

② Click Palettes in the Options bar menu. The Character palette will be displayed (see Figure 12.12).

③ Enter a value in the Tracking field. You can do this by clicking the small triangles or by typing.

A positive figure, such as 100, will widen the spacing; a negative figure, such as –50, will tighten the spacing.

Improving the spacing between characters

You can correct poor intercharacter spacing and create interesting character juxtapositions by kerning (see Figure 12.13). Like tracking, kerning is measured in one 1/1000th of an em space with unkerned spaces set at 0.

Figure 12.13 Character pairs kerned to create progressively wider spacing

Adjusting inter-character spaces

① Position the insertion point between two characters within a word. The text should not be highlighted in any way.

② Choose Character… from the Type menu. The Character palette will be displayed (see Figure 12.4).

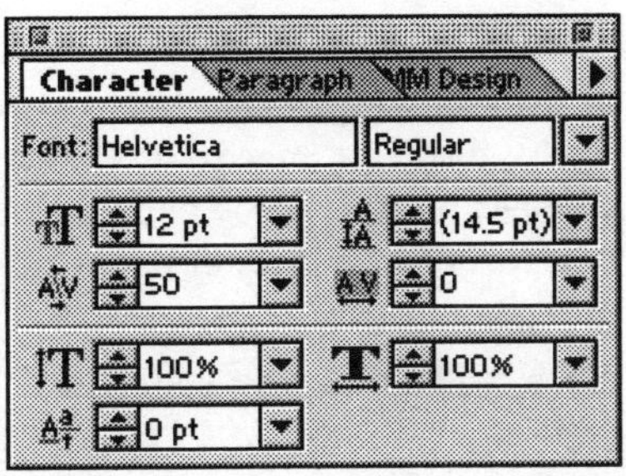

Figure 12.14 Kerning characters by 50/1000 em

③ Enter a value in the Kerning field. You can do this by clicking the small triangles or by typing.

A positive figure, such as 100, will widen the inter-character spacing; a negative figure such as –50 will tighten the inter-character spacing.

Adjusting the baseline position of text

Text can be moved up or down relative to its normal baseline position by using Baseline shift (see Figure 12.15).

① Select the text to be shifted using one of the methods described under Selecting text, page 126.

② Click Palettes in the Options bar menu. The Character palette will be displayed.

Choose Show Options in the pop-up menu if the Baseline Shift field is not showing.

③ Enter a value in the baseline Shift field (it's the field at the bottom left of the extended palette). You can do this by clicking the small triangles or by typing.

④ Press [Enter] or click the Submit button to deselect the text.

Figure 12.15 A character is shifted from its normal baseline position

Summary

Type can be added in one of two ways in Photoshop: either as point type or as paragraph type.

Point type is best for short pieces of text; paragraph type is best for column work.

Text is formatted at either a character or a paragraph level.

Each discrete piece of text, whether point type or paragraph type, occupies a layer of its own.

It's necessary to 'submit' each piece of text once you've finished working on it.

13 CREATING IMAGE COMPOSITES

Photoshop really comes into its own when creating image composites. Its layer features, guides and grids give you unparalleled control over your work whether you are developing photo-montages for print (see Figure 13.1) or complex pages for the web.

Layers are key to working with composites. They enable you to experiment freely with all sorts of adjustments and effects whilst at the same time preserving original image data.

Figure 13.1 Montage created using layers

Layers are akin to the transparent sheets of acetate used by animators in the past. They share the same resolution and image mode (RGB, CMYK and so forth) within a document so there is no need to worry about this aspect when combining images. They automatically adopt the attributes of the host document.

Layered documents are saved in native file formats Photoshop 3.0 or later or as TIFFs. Out of these only the TIFFs can be imported as layered documents by other programs, but not always reliably.

When an image is ready for use you either save the image in a suitable format, in the case of web work, or save a flattened copy in a format of your choice for print work. (There's the option to flatten the composite image itself but it's usually best to avoid doing so as the process is irreversible.)

> ! See Chapter 3, *Opening and saving images* for how to create an empty document and Chapter 5, *Altering image size and mode* for how to extend the canvas of an image.

> ▲ You can copy vector objects from Illustrator directly into Photoshop by copying and pasting or click-dragging in the same way as for raster images. The objects in the process automatically become rasterized.

Adding layers

You can create composites within existing images or from scratch within blank documents.

You add layers to a document in a number of ways, including:

- Using the New Layer controls.
- Placing, dragging and dropping, or pasting a selection or entire image into a host document.
- Adding shapes using the pen or shape tools.
- Adding type using the type tool.

Adding and naming a new blank layer

① Hold down [Alt] and click the New Layer button at the bottom of the Layers palette (see Figure 13.2). The Layer Options dialog box will be displayed.

② Name the layer. Click OK.

Figure 13.2 Creating a new blank layer

▲ When creating composites for web images and pages, ensure that the resolution of the composite document is 72 ppi.

Placing an entire image

① Choose Place… from the File menu. The Place directory dialog box will be displayed.

② Use the directory dialog box controls to locate your file. Click Place.

Dragging and dropping a selection or entire image

① Select the whole image or the part of the image you wish to use.

② With the Move tool selected, click-drag the image into the window of the host document. It will be pasted onto a new layer above the previously active layer (or background layer). If a new layer is already present, empty and active, it will be pasted on this layer.

Copying a layer from another document

● Click-drag the layer from the Layers palette into the window of the host document. It will be added to the palette in the host document.

Pasting a selection or entire images

① Select the whole image or the part of the image you wish to use. Choose Copy or Cut from the Edit menu (see Figure 13.3).

② If you wish to paste within another document, move to that document. Otherwise skip this step.

③ Choose Paste from the Edit menu. The image will be pasted onto a new layer above the previously active layer (or background layer). If a new layer is already present, empty and active, it will be pasted on this layer.

! An image pasted into another document will take on the resolution of the host document, resulting in a change of dimensions of the pasted image if the resolutions differ.

Figure 13.3 A cut selection exposes the current background colour

Adding shapes using the pen or shape tools

When you add shapes in a new colour, a new shape layer is created together with a layer clipping path (see Figure 3.4). The clipping path acts as a mask so that the layer colour only appears within the shapes themselves. See Chapter 11 for how to work with shape layers.

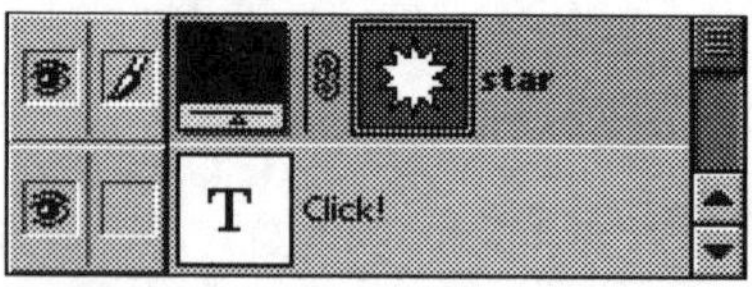

Figure 13.4 How shape and type layers appear in the Layers palette

Adding type using the type tool

When you add pieces of type, a new text layer is created. The first few words provide the name for the layer (see Figure 3.4). See Chapter 12 for how to work with type layers.

Organizing layers

Renaming layers

① Hold down [Alt] and double-click layer name in Layers palette. The Layer Properties dialog box is displayed.

② Rename the layer. Click OK.

Changing the order of layers

● Click-drag the layer up or down within the Layers palette (see Figure 13.5).

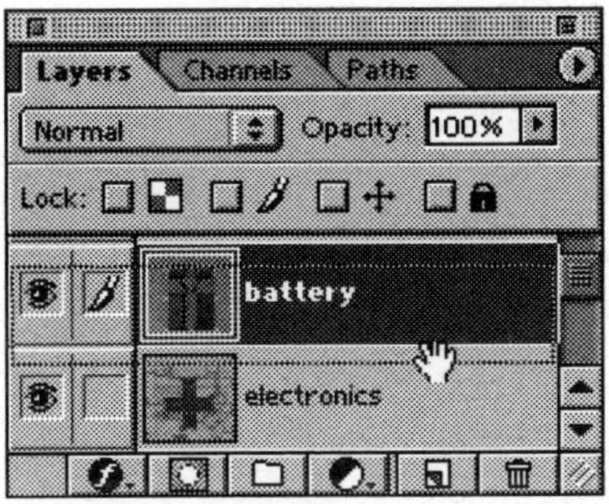

Figure 13.5 Reordering layers

Linking layers

You can fix the spatial relationship between two or more layers by linking them.

① Select the layer you wish to link to in the Layer palette.

② Click in the blank square to the left of another layer name. A link icon will appear. This layer is now linked to the first layer (see Figure 13.6).

③ Repeat step 2 to link other layers to the first layer.

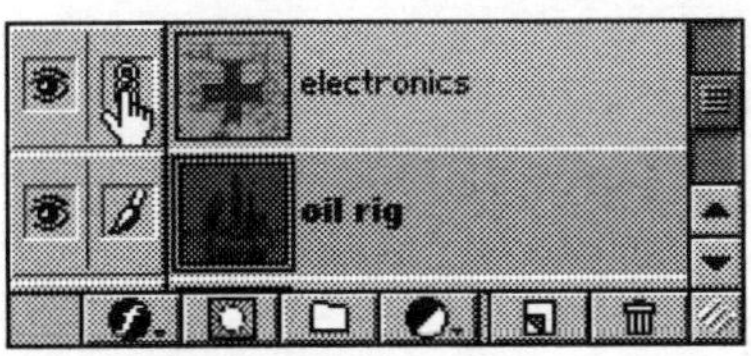

Figure 13.6 Linking layers

Unlinking layers

① Select the layer you wish to unlink from in the Layer palette.

② Click on the link icon to the left of the layer name you wish to unlink. A link icon will be removed. This layer is now unlinked.

③ Repeat step 2 to unlink other layers.

Collating layers into sets

By grouping layers together, you can more easily move multiple layers up or down the stacking order. You can also apply attributes or a mask to a group of layers and collapse a group to free up space in the Layers palette.

① Link the layers you wish to group into a set.

② Choose Layer Set from Linked from the New… sub-menu in the Layer menu.

Creating a new layer set

① Hold down [Alt] and click the New Layer Set button at the bottom of the Layers palette. The Layer Set dialog box will be displayed.

② Name the layer set. Click OK.

Choosing a mode for a layer set

① Select the layer set.

② Choose Pass Through from the mode pop-up menu (see Figure 13.7).

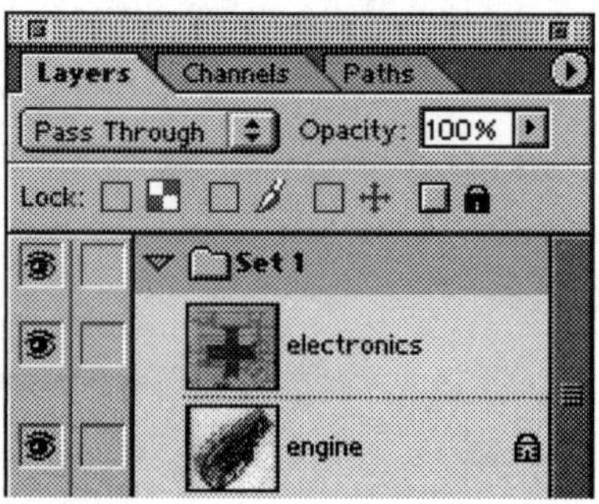

Figure 13.7 Layer palette displaying a layer set

Pass Through allows the blending modes of individual layers to operate in the normal way.

Renaming layer sets

① Hold down [Alt] and double-click layer set name in the Layers palette. The Layer Set Properties dialog box is displayed.

② Rename the layer set. Click OK.

Deleting a layer set

① Select the layer set you wish to delete.

② Click the Wastebasket button in the Layers palette.

Moving a layer in and out of a layer set

- Click-drag the layer out of the folder into either another folder or on a level by itself in the layers palette.

Locking layers

You can lock layers so that they are either fully or partially protected from changes: you can prevent a layer from being moved by the Move tool or cursor keys, you can prevent pixellated areas from being changed and you can preserve the transparency of layers.

① Select the layer you wish to be protected.

Either:

② Check Lock All to fully lock a layer (see Figure 13.8).

Or:

② Check Lock Image Pixels, Lock Transparent Pixels and/or Lock Position to lock these attributes individually.

Figure 13.8 Locking layers

- ▲ If you Uncheck Lock Transparent Pixels and paint with a brush set to Behind mode you can paint behind layers.

Unlocking layers

① Select the layer you wish to be unlocked.

② Uncheck the Lock All box icon to fully unlock a layer or uncheck the Lock Position box icon.

Deleting layers

① Select the layer you wish to delete.

② Click the Wastebasket button in the Layers palette (see Figure 13.9).

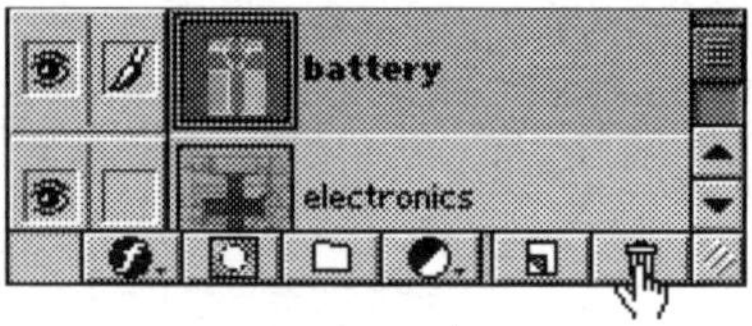

Figure 13.9 Deleting a layer

Converting layers

Converting a background into a layer

Unlike normal layers the position of a background layer in the stacking order cannot be changed – it must remain at the bottom – nor can any modes or opacity settings be applied to it without firstly converting it into a normal layer.

① Double-click the background layer thumbnail in the Layers palette. The New Layer dialog box will be displayed.

② Name the layer and press .

Converting a layer into a background

You can convert a layer into a background in a layer-only document.

① Select the layer you wish to convert.

② Choose New Background from Layer in the New sub-menu in the Layers menu.

③ Select the layer you wish to convert into a background.

Converting a layer into a fill layer

You can fill a blank layer with colour by converting it into a fill layer.

① Select the layer you wish to convert.

② Choose either Solid Colour, Gradient or Pattern from the New Fill Layer sub-menu in the Layers menu. The New Layer dialog box will be displayed.

③ Name the layer and click OK. In the case of Solid Colour, the Colour Picker will be displayed (refer to page 47). In the case of Gradient Fill, the Gradient Fill dialog will be displayed (refer to page 51). In the case of Pattern Fill, the Pattern Fill dialog will be displayed.

④ Choose your settings. Click OK. The new layer with linked layer mask will appear in the Layers palette.

Altering layer mode and opacity

Altering layer mode

- Choose an option from the Mode pop-up menu (see Figure 13.10).

  See Blending modes (page 151) to learn how they affect image blending.

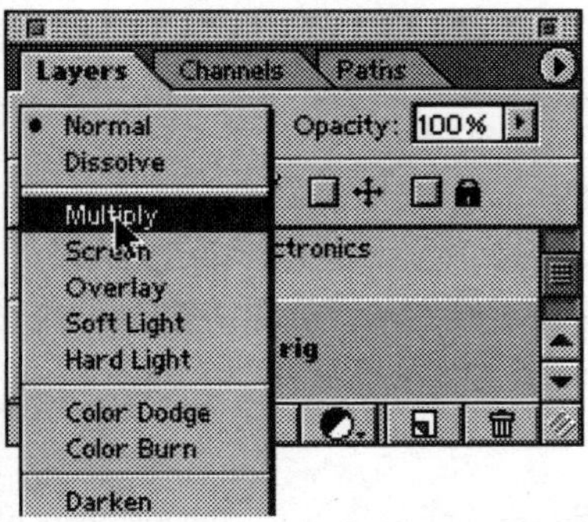

Figure 13.10 Changing the mode of a layer

Altering layer opacity

You can alter the opacity of a layer by moving the slider on the Layers palette (see Figure 13.11).

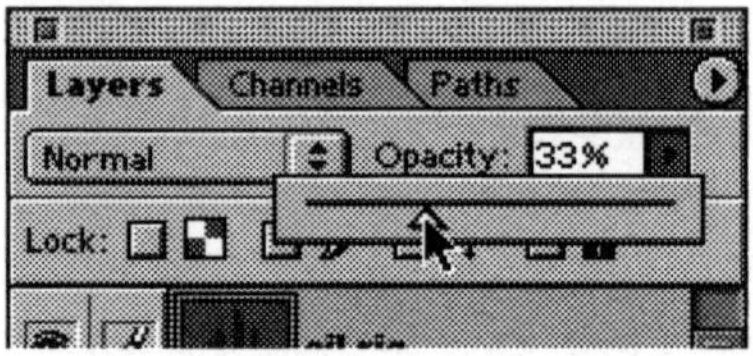

Figure 13.11 Changing the opacity of a layer

Applying adjustments to layers

You can experiment with tonal and colour adjustments on a layer-by-layer basis by using adjustment layers. Adjustments applied this way are previewed only. Image data therefore remains unmodified.

① Select the layer you wish to adjust.

② Choose an option from the New Adjustment Layer submenu in the Layers menu. The New Layer dialog box will be displayed.

③ Check Group with Previous Layer if you wish to restrict the adjustment to the layer selected in step 1. If you wish you can do this later within the Layers menu.

④ Click OK. The appropriate adjustment dialog box will be displayed.

⑤ Make adjustments as necessary (see Chapter 10 on the use of the controls).

⑥ Click OK. The new adjustment layer with linked layer mask will appear in the Layers palette above the previously selected layer. If the new adjustment layer was grouped with the previous layer the thumbnail will appear indented.

⑦ Repeat all steps to add additional adjustment layers.

! When an adjustment layer lies above another layer, it uses the effect of the lower adjustment layer as its starting point.

▲ If you wish to permanently implement an adjustment carried out this way, 'merge down' the adjustment layer. See Merging layers (page 150).

Accessing adjustment dialog boxes

● Double-click the layer thumbnail in the Layers palette.

Working on layers

Selecting layers

● Click on the layer thumbnail in the Layers palette (see Figure 13.12).

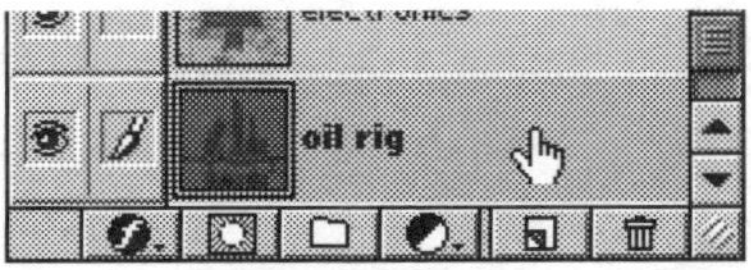

Figure 13.12 Selecting a layer

Or:

① Select the Move tool in the toolbox. Check Auto Select Layer in the Options bar (see Figure 13.13).

② Click on pixellated area within image composite. The layer will automatically be selected.

Figure 13.13 The Move tool options

Or:

● With the Move tool selected, choose a layer from the context-sensitive menu. See Selecting options from context-sensitive menus in Chapter 2.

! The selected layer is always identified by the presence of a paint brush icon.

Selecting pixellated areas only

① Select the layer.

② Hold down [⌘] and click on the layer thumbnail. The pixellated areas will be selected.

The selection border is located on the currently selected layer.

! Temporarily unlock the layer above if this keystroke doesn't work.

Selecting text on text layers

- Double-click the text layer thumbnail in the Layer palette. Both the text and Type tool will be selected.

Deleting pixellated areas

- Click-drag over the selected layer using the Eraser tool.

  Or:

- Make a selection and press [Delete].

Filling areas

① Choose a suitable background colour.

② Make a selection.

③ Hold down [⌘] and press [Delete].

Floating images

You can move and copy selections without creating new layers.

① Select the part of the image you wish to move.

② With the Move tool active, click-drag the selection. Hold down [Alt] to copy a selection. The image will become a floating selection.

③ Adjust its opacity and blending mode, as necessary.

④ Choose Deselect from the Select menu.

✚ A moved selection exposes the current background colour.

Pasting into selection borders

① Cut or copy a selection.

② Make a selection.

③ Choose Paste Into from the Edit menu. A new layer and layer mask will be created: the pasted image will appear on the new layer, the selection border will be represented by a white area within the layer mask.

Removing fringe colours

Pasted images sometimes include unwanted colours around their edges. You can replace these fringe pixels by nearby pure colours.

① Choose Defringe… from the Matting sub-menu in the Layer menu. The Defringe dialog box will be displayed.

② Enter a value in the Width field.

③ Click OK.

Gradating images

You can easily experiment with image gradations by using layer masks.

Adding a layer mask

① Select the layer in the Layer palette you wish to mask.

② Choose Reveal All from the Add Layer Mask sub-menu in the Layers palette menu. A layer mask thumbnail appears to the right of the Layer thumbnail. It is automatically linked and selected.

③ Select the Gradient tool. Choose the black and white option from the pop-up Gradient picker in the Options bar.

④ Click-drag over the area of the layer to be gradated (see Figure 13.14). The effect will be immediately previewed (see Figure 13.15).

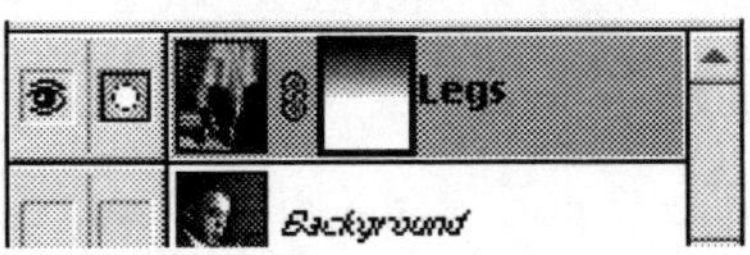

Figure 13.14 Layer with linked layer mask. The mask icon to the left of the layer thumbnail indicates that the layer mask is selected.

▲ You can switch between the mask and its accompanying layer at any time, by clicking on either thumbnail in the layers palette.

✚ The current foreground and background colours will automatically revert to black and white whilst the layer mask is selected.

Figure 13.15 Image gradated using a layer mask

Applying or discarding a layer mask

You can apply a layer mask or discard it at any time.

① Select the mask.

② Choose Apply or Discard from the Remove Layer Mask sub-menu in the Layer menu.

Using layer styles

You can apply style effects to layers whether they are ordinary layers, text layers or shape layers.

① Select a layer.

② Choose an option (from Drop Shadow through to Stroke) from the Layer Style sub-menu in the Layer menu. The Layer Style dialog box will be displayed.

③ Choose settings in the centre region of the dialog box. Ensure Preview is Checked or ticked so you can view the result (see Figure 13.16).

④ If you wish to apply an additional style, select the style from the Styles list on the left of the dialog box and repeat step 3.

⑤ Click OK once you have completed your settings.

Figure 13.16 Layer effects: drop shadow, bevel and emboss and satin (top row); drop shadow, stroke and pattern overlay (bottom row)

Creating borders

Although not strictly layer attributes I include two techniques that are often used in image composites.

Borders are created in one of two ways in Photoshop. You can create a vignetted (soft-edged) border using the Border command or a hard or soft-edged edge stroke using the Stroke command.

The edges of a stroke are defined by the aliasing of the selection around which its formed. A stroke also has positional and blending attributes that a border hasn't.

Selecting a border surrounding a selection

① Choose Border… from the Modify sub-menu of the Select menu. The Border dialog box will be displayed (see Figure 13.17).

② Enter a value in the Width field.

③ Click OK.

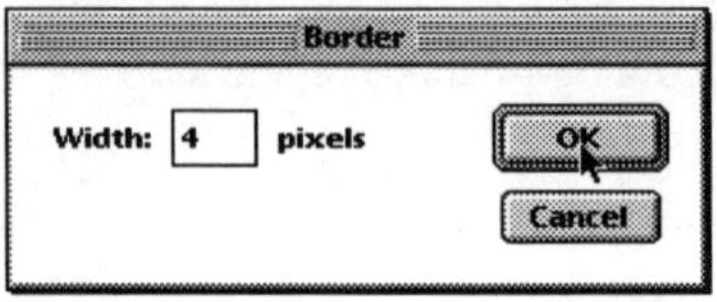

Figure 13.17 The Border dialog box

Creating a stroke around a selection or layer

① Choose Stroke… from the Edit menu. The Stroke dialog box will be displayed.

② Enter a value in the Width field.

③ Select an option under Location.

④ Enter a value in the Opacity field and choose an option from the Mode pop-up menu.

⑤ Click OK.

Transforming images

You can scale, rotate, skew, distort, flip or apply perspective to selections using the Free Transform or Transform commands.

Both commands allow you to switch between transformations 'on the fly', i.e. you can preview a series of effects without implementing each in turn. This speeds the transformation process and – more importantly – it results in less image degradation.

Resampling invariably takes place during a transformation, resulting in pixels being added or deleted. Extreme transformations will undoubtedly result in loss of image detail.

Using either Transform command

① Select a layer or make a selection.

② Choose either Transform or Free Transform from the Edit menu. Handles will be added to the selection border.

③ Click-drag a corner handle to scale the selection and/or click drag around the outside of the selection border to rotate it.

④ Move the pointer to one of the handles of the transform border and access the context-sensitive pop-up menu to choose further transform commands.

⑤ Repeat step 4 for each additional transformation.

⑥ Press [Enter] to implement the transformation or press [Esc] to abort (see Figure 13.8).

▲ If you choose Free Transform you can switch between transformations using the modifier keys. Hold down the Command key to distort a selection, the Command and Alt keys to skew a selection (using a side handle) and the Command, Alt and Shift keys to create a perspective with the selection.

You can transform groups of layers by linking them first.

Figure 13.18 A transformed image

Merging and flattening layers

If you are using a lot of layers within a document, merge those that needn't remain separate, if only to reduce the document size and speed processing times.

When your composite work is complete, all layers will finally need to be flattened (integrated with the background) for print output. This is best done to a copy of an image rather than the original, so you can return to the unflattened version should you need to revise it.

If you have created an composite for the web, always leave the layers intact so that you are able to make use of the flexibility they offer.

There are two main differences between merging layers and flattening an image:

- A merged transparent background retains its transparency whilst the background of a flattened image always becomes opaque.
- Flattened documents discard their invisible layers, merged layers have no effect on other layers.

Merging layers

Use this process to merge a layer with an underlying layer.

① Click on the layer name or thumbnail in the Layers palette (if not already selected).

② Choose Merge Down from the Layer menu.

! When merged, pasted layers assume the opacity and mode of the layer with which they are merged.

Flattening an image

Either:

① Make visible only those layers (including the background) you wish to include in the flattened image.

② Choose Flatten Image from the Layers palette pop-up menu. An alert box saying 'Discard hidden layers?' will be displayed if any layers are invisible. Click OK.

Or:

- Follow the procedure for saving a flattened copy of a document in Chapter 3.

! Layers are automatically flattened when an image is converted from RGB to another mode, such as CMYK.

Blending modes

The blending modes control the way blend colours affect base colours.

The base colour is the original image colour. The blend colour is the colour being applied to the image by a paint tool, command or layer.

Normal/Threshold Blend colours fully replace base colours. This is the usual mode.

Dissolve Base and blend colours are randomly mixed to create a result based on the opacity at any pixel location.

Behind Similar to Normal, except blend colours only affect transparent areas. Available if Lock Transparency is unchecked in the Layers palette.

Clear Creates transparency. Available for the Line and Paintbucket tools and for the fill and stroke commands, provided Lock Transparency is unchecked in the Layers palette.

Multiply Multiplies blend colours with base colours. The result is similar to overlaying transparencies on a light box or blending colours with transparent markers.

Screen Multiplies the inverse of the blend and base colours. The result is similar to projecting multiple transparencies on a screen.

Overlay Multiplies or screens depending on the base colour, maintaining the lightness and darkness of the base image.

Soft Light Darkens or lightens depending on the blend colour. The result is similar to shining a diffused spotlight on the image.

Hard Light Multiplies or screens depending on the blend colour. The result is similar to shining a harsh spotlight on the image.

Colour Dodge Brightens to reflect the blend colour.

Colour Burn Darkens to reflect the blend colour.

Darken Changes base colours lighter than the blend colour.

Lighten Changes base colours darker than the blend colour. The result is similar to reflections in a window.

Difference Subtracts the blend colour from the base colour and vice versa depending on which has the greater brightness value.

Exclusion Similar to Difference but the result is less contrasty.

Hue Changes the hue of base colours; luminance and saturation levels remain unaltered.

Saturation Changes the saturation of base colours; hue and luminance levels remain unaltered.

Colour Changes the hue and saturation of base colours; luminosity levels remain unaltered. This mode is perfect for colouring monochrome and tinting colour images.

Luminosity Changes the luminosity of base colours; the inverse of Colour.

Summary

Composite images are effectively multi-layered documents, with each layer being a component image.

Layers are automatically added to documents when you paste images or when you create text or draw shapes.

The opacity and blending mode of images can be set on a layer-by-layer basis.

Layers masks enable you to gradate images whilst adjustment layers enable you to enhance images on a layer-by-layer basis.

The transform functions enable you to scale, flip, skew, rotate and distort images.

It's best to keep layers intact; only flattening them in copies of documents.

14 CREATING WEB PAGES

Slicing composites for the web

In the previous chapter I showed you how you can create complex image composites. Here I take you through the web features of Photoshop and its companion program ImageReady. The two programs in combination allow you to create, with relative ease, feature-rich, interactive pages for web sites.

When you are creating a page for the web, you need to divide the document's canvas – its image area – into slices, add interactive links and maybe HTML text, and optimize the slices for fast downloading (see Figure 14.1).

When you save an image for the web, you can choose to generate an HTML file complete with text, JavaScript and links to the resulting GIF, JPEG or PNF image files.

Figure 14.1 Part of a web page composite sliced ready for saving as an HTML document

Slices divide the image canvas into functional areas. Each slice is saved as an independent file that contains its own settings, colour palette, links, rollover and animation effects (the latter two effects only achievable in ImageReady).

The slices you define yourself are called user-slices; the slices you create from layers are called layer-based slices. Slices automatically created to account for the remaining areas of the image canvas are called auto-slices. A further type of slice, called subslices, is generated where slices overlap.

When covering slicing I guide you through the controls of both programs. Only when a control is unavailable in Photoshop do I refer to ImageReady alone.

! See Creating a blank document in Chapter 3 for optimum canvas sizes for web pages.

! See Saving sliced images in Chapter 3 for saving web composites.

Switching between Photoshop and ImageReady

● In Photoshop click the Jump to ImageReady button at the bottom of the toolbox. In ImageReady click the Jump to Photoshop button at the same location.

✚ If either program has not already been loaded on the RAM it will now be loaded. Its title and menu bar will be displayed in a few moments along with the document window.

Slicing up an image

Creating slices

Creating user-slices

① Select the Slice tool in either program.

② Choose Normal from the Style pop-up menu in the Options bar/palette.

③ Click-drag diagonally over the area to be sliced.

▲ In ImageReady, you can create slices from selection borders or from guides using commands in its Slices menu.

Creating layer-based slices

Layer-based slices encompass the pixellated part of a layer and are especially useful for rollovers. If you move or increase the size of the pixellated area of a layer by applying a style, for instance, the slice adjusts its position and/or size accordingly.

① Select the layer.

② Choose New Layer-based Slice from the Layer menu in either program.

Converting slices

Converting auto-slices into user-slices

Auto-slices are linked and share optimizations settings. If you wish to alter the setting of an individual slice without affecting others, you must first convert it into a user-slice.

① With the Slice Select tool active, select an Auto-slice.

② In ImageReady choose Promote to User Slice(s) from its Slices menu.

In Photoshop click the Promote to User Slice button in its Options bar (see Figure 14.2).

Figure 14.2 Slice Select tool options

Converting layer-based slices into user-slices

① With the Slice Select tool active, select a layer-based slice.

② In ImageReady choose Promote to User Slice(s) from its Slices menu.

In Photoshop click the Promote to User Slice button in the Options bar.

Viewing slices

Outlines

Slice lines define the boundary of slices. Solid lines indicate that a slice is either a user- or layer-based slice; dotted lines indicate that a slice is an auto-slice.

Colours

Slice colours indicate whether a slice is a user- or layer-based slice or an auto-slice. User-/layer-based slices by default are blue whereas auto-slices are grey.

Numbers

Slices are numbered from left to right and from top to bottom. The numbers are updated when the arrangement and number of slices is altered.

Symbols

Symbols indicate whether a user-slice is an image or not, whether a slice is layer based, whether a slice is linked or whether a slice includes a rollover effect (see Figure 14.3).

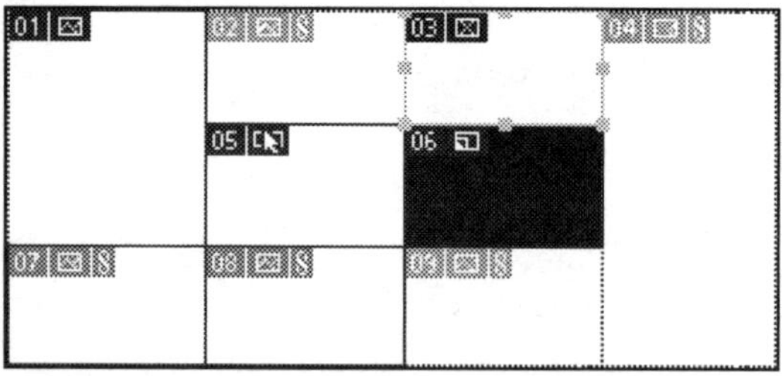

Figure 14.3 Slice identification: 01 is a user slice, 02, 04, 07, 08 and 09 are linked auto-slices, 03 is a user slice with no image, 05 is a rollover slice and 06 is a layer slice

Showing/hiding slices

- Choose Slices from the Show sub-menu in the View menu to tick/untick the command.

Snapping/unsnapping slices to guides

- Choose Guides from the Snap to sub-menu in the View menu to tick/untick the command.

! Ensure Snap is ticked in the View menu for the snapping to occur.

Working with slices

Selecting a slice

- With the Slice Select tool active, click on slice.

▲ Hold down the Command key to switch between the Slice tool and the Slice Select tool in either program.

▲ Select multiple slices in ImageReady by holding down the Shift key and clicking on slices or by click-dragging from within an auto-slice across other slices.

Moving a user slice

● With the Slice Select tool active, click-drag slice.

Resizing a user-slice

① With the Slice Select tool active, click on slice.

② Click-drag a side or corner handle.

! In ImageReady common edges are resized accordingly.

Arranging slices

You can change the stacking order of overlapping user- and layer-based slices.

① With the Slice Select tool active, click on slice.

② Click a stacking order button in the Options bar (see Figure 14.4).

Figure 14.4 Slice Select tool options in Photoshop

Aligning slices

You can align user-based slices in ImageReady to reduce the number of auto-slices and thus create more streamlined HTML files.

① With the Slice Select tool active, select the user-slices you wish to align.

② Click an align option in the Options bar (see Figure 14.5).

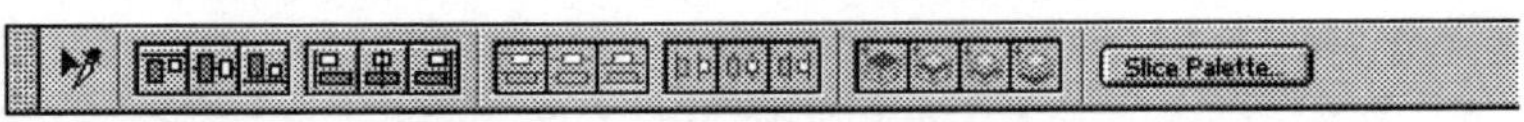

Figure 14.5 Slice Select tool options in ImageReady

Deleting a user-slice

① With the Slice Select tool active, click on slice.

② Press Delete.

Deleting all user- and layer-based slices

- Choose Clear Slices from the View menu in Photoshop and Delete All from the Slices menu in ImageReady.

Adding HTML text to a slice

① With the Slice Select tool active, click on slice.

② Double-click a slice in Photoshop. The Slice Options dialog box will be displayed.

③ Choose No Image in the Slice Type pop-up menu.

④ Enter text in the HTML Field including, if you wish, standard HTML tags (see Figure 14.6).

⑤ Press ↵ .

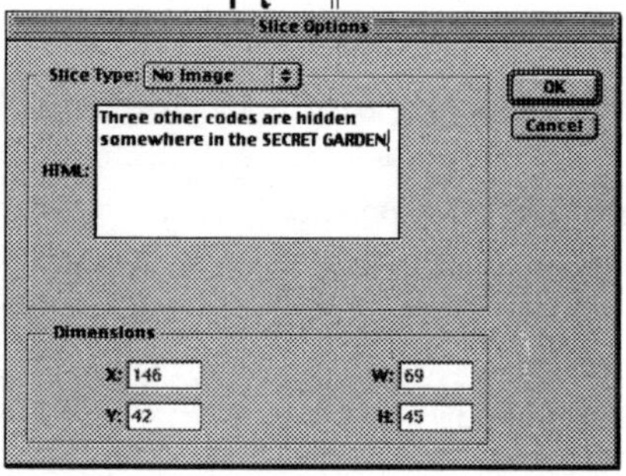

Figure 14.6 The HTML field in the Slice Options dialog box

! In ImageReady the Slices palette takes the place of the Slice Options dialog box. Within the extended version of the palette you can specify the vertical and horizontal alignment of text within pop-up menus.

! Avoid entering more text than a slice can accommodate as excess text will alter cell sizes and upset the overall table structure. Note that HTML text will only show when you preview the page within a browser.

Assigning a URL to a slice

① With the Slice Select tool active, click on slice.

② Double-click a slice in Photoshop. The Slice Options dialog box will be displayed.

③ Choose Image in the Slice Type pop-up menu.

④ Enter appropriate information in the remaining fields.

⑤ Press ↵ .

! In ImageReady the Slices palette takes the place of the Slice Options dialog box.

Optimizing slices

Slices are optimized by using the Save for Web dialog box in Photoshop or by using the Optimize and Colour Table palettes in ImageReady.

Deselected slices appear dimmed in both contexts, with user- and layer-based slices appearing brighter than auto-slices. Selected slices appear at normal brightness for optimization purposes.

Optimizing a slice

① With the Slice Select tool active, select slice(s). The slice(s) will revert to normal brightness.

② Follow the instructions as described in Chapter 15: Optimizing images for the web.

! Multiple slices can be selected only in ImageReady.

Linking and unlinking slices

Linking slices

In ImageReady you can link slices so that they share optimization settings. This saves time and ensures consistency between slices containing similar image content.

① With the Slice Select tool active, select two or more slices.

② Choose Link Slices from the Slices menu.

! If the first slice you select is a user-slice, any auto-slice you link to the slice will become a user-slice. If the first slice you select is an auto-slice, any user-slice you link to the slice will be linked to the auto-slices.

Unlinking a slice from a set

① With the Slice Select tool active, select a linked slice.

② Choose Unlink Slices from the Slices menu.

Unlinking all slices in a set

① With the Slice Select tool active, select a linked slice.

② Choose Unlink Set from the Slices menu.

Creating image maps

In ImageReady you can set multiple-linked areas, called image map areas, with each area linking to a different file. Unlike slices, these areas need not be rectangular; in fact they can be any shape you wish. They can also overlap slice bounderies.

Image maps are either tool- or layer-based. Tool-based image maps can be rectangular, circular or even polygonal.

Layer-based image maps on the other hand are defined by the pixellated part of a layer. They are particularly useful when combined with rollover effects. If you increase the size of the pixellated area by applying a style, such as a drop shadow for instance, the image map automatically resizes to suit.

Figure 14.7 Rectangular and polygonal image maps (shown selected)

Creating a tool-based image map

① Select one of the image map tools in the toolbox.

② Check Fixed Size in the Options bar and enter whole number (pixel) values in the Width and Height fields or leave unchecked (see Figure 14.8). Not available for the Polygon tool.

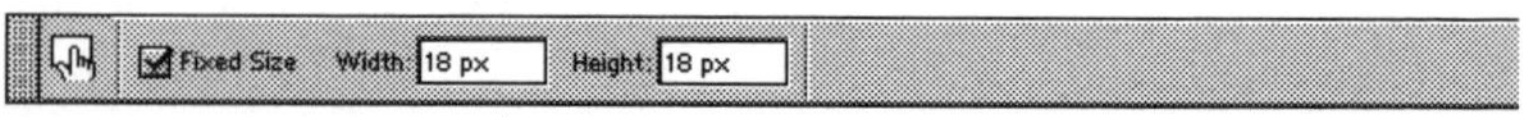

Figure 14.8 Image Map tool options

③ Click-drag in a diagonal direction to define the image map area. In the case of the Polygon tool (see Figure 14.7), click to define the corners points of a shape. Finally click the starting point. (A small circle will appear beside the cursor to denote it's over the first point.)

Creating an image map from a layer

① Select the layer from which to create an image map area.

② Choose New Layer Based Image Map Area from the Layer menu.

Converting layer-based image maps into tool-based image maps

Since layer-based image maps are defined by layer content, it's only possible to change their areas by image editing. By converting them to tool-based image maps, you can alter their scale independently of image content.

① With the Image Map Select tool active, select a layer-based image map area.

② Choose Promote Layer Based Image Map Area from the pop-up menu in the Image Map palette.

Showing/hiding image maps

- Click the Image Map Visibility button in the toolbox.

Selecting image maps

- With the Image Map Select tool active, click on image map area.

Moving image maps

- With the Image Map Select tool active, click-drag image map area.

Resizing image maps

① With the Image Map Select tool active, select rectangular or circular image map area.

② Enter values (in pixels) in the X, Y, W(idth), H(eight) and R(adius) fields in the Image Map palette (see Figure 14.9).

! X specifies the distance between the left edge of a rectangle or the centre of a circle and the ruler origin point. Y specifies the distance between the top edge of a rectangle or the centre of a circle and the ruler origin point.

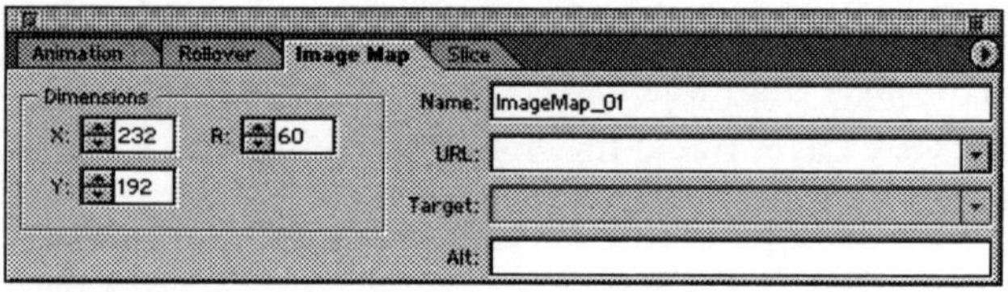

Figure 14.9 The dimension fields in the Image Map palette

Reshaping layer-based image maps

Layer-based image map areas, which by default are rectangular, can be given different shapes.

① With the Image Map Select tool active, select the layer-based image map area.

② Choose an option from the Shape pop-up menu in the Image Map palette.

Arranging image maps

You can change the stacking order of image maps.

① With the Image Map Select tool active, select one or more image map areas.

② Click a stacking order button in the Options bar (see Figure 14.10).

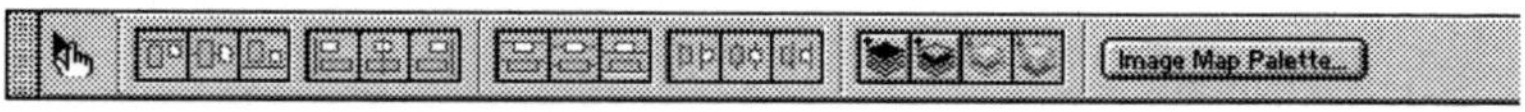

Figure 14.10 Image Map Select tool options

Deleting an image map

① With the Image Map Select tool active, select the image map area.

② Press Delete.

Specifying links

① With the Image Map Select tool active, select the image map area.

② Enter a URL into the URL field. The URL must begin with http:// (see Figure 14.11).

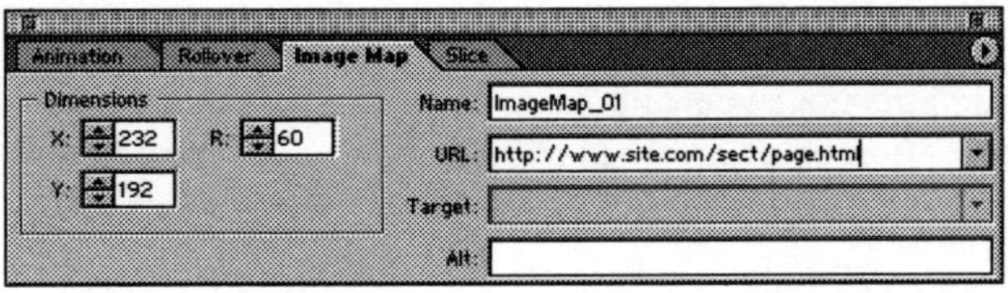

Figure 14.11 Entering a URL in the Image Map palette

③ Enter appropriate information in remaining fields.

Creating rollovers

Rollovers are a web effect in which different states of an image appear when a viewer performs a mouse action. They are mostly used for buttons. When you pass the cursor over a rollover button, the button changes appearance, when you hold down the mouse button, it changes again and so on. Each appearance is effectively a state.

You can use a slice or an image map area for a rollover. By default, each has only one state – the Normal state, seen in the browser when the image is first loaded.

When you add a new rollover state, by default it starts off as a duplicate of the previous state. However, you can use a different layer for a new state by hiding the previously visible layer and showing a new layer (see Figure 14.12). Since rollover states must all be the same size ensure that image content remains within slice boundaries.

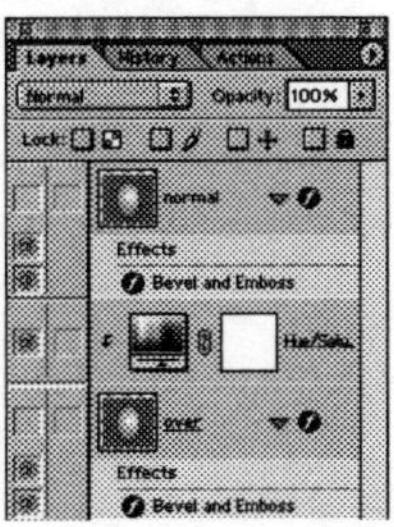

Figure 14.12 Layers dedicated to individual button states

When you save an image with rollover states, each state is saved as a separate image file. By default, rollover states are named after the slice name with the relevant mouse action appended to the name.

Working with rollovers

It's best to position the image content for rollovers on layers of their own and to lock the position of all layers to avoid unintentional image movements.

Creating rollover states

① With the appropriatc tool active, select the layer-based slice or layer-based image map area.

② Click the New State button in the Rollover palette (see Figure 14.13).

③ Choose a rollover state from the pop-up menu immediately above the rollover thumbnail or leave as is.

④ Modify the image using the Layers palette.

⑤ Repeat steps 3–4 for further states, if required.

⑥ Reselect the Normal state once you have finished.

▲ Changes made outside the area of a selected slice are included within rollover states even though they don't appear within rollover thumbnails.

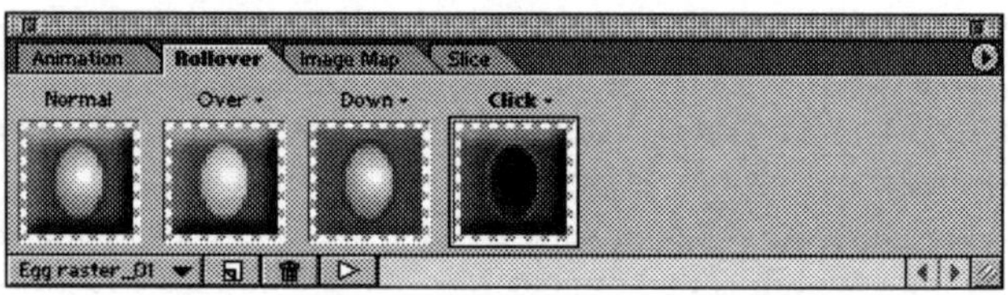

Figure 14.13 The Rollover palette showing four button states

Previewing rollover states

Either:

① Click the Rollover Preview button in ImageReady's toolbox.

Or:

① Click the Play button in the Rollover palette.

② Perform mouse actions to test the rollover effect.

Deleting rollover states

① Select the rollover state in the Rollover palette.

② Click the Wastebasket button.

Creating animations

You can create simple multi-frame animations within ImageReady without having to resort to a dedicated animation program.

Animations are sequences of images, or frames, that are displayed over time. When viewed in quick succession, the illusion of movement is created.

You can create each frame by yourself or use the tween feature to create a succession of intermediate frames that vary a layer's opacity, position and effects. You can also optimize frames, and specify looping.

Furthermore, animations can also be associated with different rollover states.

Working with animations

It's best to position image content for frames on layers of their own. This allows you to use the layer commands and options to change the position and appearance of an image across a series of frames. Using layer attributes to modify frames not only simplifies the animation process but also enables you to edit animations more easily once they have been saved. It's also wise to lock the position of layers you don't plan to move.

The first frame of an animation is based on the current state of an image. When you add a frame it starts off as a duplicate of the previous frame (in this case the first frame). You then change the state of the frame by hiding/showing layers and/or modifying image content before adding the next frame (see Figure 14.14).

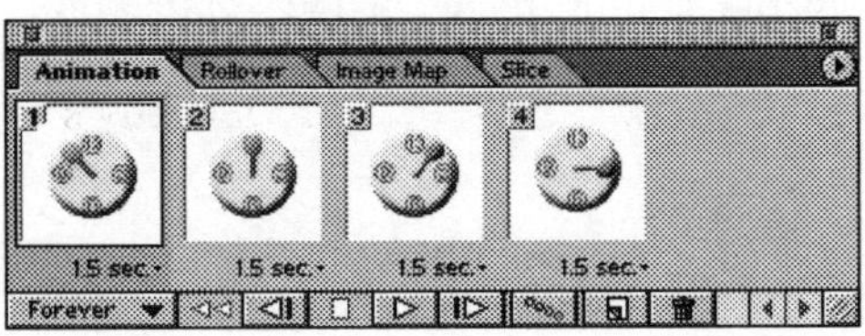

Figure 14.14 The Animation palette showing four frames

Changes you make to frames are either frame-specific or global. Those you make by using the Layer palette commands and options, including a layer's opacity, blending mode, visibility, position, layer masks, clipping paths and layer effects, are frame-specific. Changes you make to vector content and pixel content using the painting and editing tools, adjust controls, filters and type tool, however, are global.

When you save an image with animations, each frame is saved as a separate image file, By default, animation frames are named after the slice name with the relevant mouse action, if applicable, appended to the name.

Adding animation frames

- Click the New Frame button in the Animation palette (see Figure 14.14).

! If you plan to create a new layer each time you add a frame, choose Add layer to New Frames from the pop-up menu in the Animation palette to tick the command.

Selecting a frame

- Select frame thumbnail in the Animation palette.

Selecting multiple frames

- Hold down [Shift] and click on frame thumbnails in the Animation palette.

Changing the order of a frame

- Click-drag the frame thumbnail in the Animation palette.

Deleting a frame

- Select frame and click on Wastebasket button.

Deleting entire animation

- Choose Delete from the pop-up menu in the Animation palette.

Tweening frames

① Select a single frame or multiple contiguous frames.

② Click the Tween button in the Animation palette. The Tween dialog box will be displayed.

③ Select All Layers or Selected Layer.

④ Select Position to tween movement, Opacity to tween opacity, and Effects to tween layer effects.

⑤ Choose an option from the Tween With menu.

⑥ Enter a value in the Frames to Add field.

⑦ Click OK. The new frames will be added to the Animation palette.

Looping an animation

- Choose an option from the Looping pop-up menu below the first frame thumbnail.

Timing frames

- Choose an option from the Delay pop-up menus below each frame thumbnail.

Discarding frames

When displaying frames, current frames are either discarded before moving onto the next frame or kept to show beneath transparent areas.

① Select frame(s).

② Press to choose an option from the context-sensitive menu.

Flattening frames into layers

You can flatten an animation into layers with each layer representing a different frame. Original layers are preserved and can be made visible for further frame production, if necessary.

- Choose Flatten Frames for the pop-up menu in the Layers palette.

Playing animations

- Click the Play button in the Animation palette.
- Click the Stop button to stop and the Rewind button to rewind the animation.

Previewing web pages

- Click the Preview in Default Browser button in ImageReady's toolbox.

Summary

Web page composites need to be sliced into discrete image areas prior to optimization.

Optimization involves a trade off between fast download times and image quality.

'No image' slices can be specified as table cells containing HTML text and tags.

Image maps allow you to create shaped interactive areas within image slices.

Rollovers are created by developing different button states often involving layer effects.

Simple animations are created by creating a sequence of frames containing different images.

15 PREPARING IMAGES FOR PRODUCTION

Photoshop documents need to be in the correct mode and appropriate file formats before they can be inserted into host documents, whatever the target medium.

The mode will be determined by the delivery medium and colour availability, i.e. whether images are to be printed or viewed on screen and how many, and which colours are to be used.

The choice of file format is limited by what a host document can accept. Depending on their purpose, format types take into account such factors as colour fidelity, image quality, file size and data transfer/decompression times.

For printed images Bitmap, greyscale, duotone and CMYK are the standard modes with TIFF and EPS the main formats. For screen images RGB is the standard mode with PICT, JPEG, GIF and PNG some of the more popular formats.

Four of the formats just mentioned employ compression alogorithms to reduce file sizes and to improve data transfer times: GIF and TIFF use the LZW algorithm (in the case of TIFF it's a user option); JPEG has its own compression system which is described as lossy, whilst the LZW system is lossless; data is lost in the former to achieve its very high levels of compression. PNG employs a lossless algorithm not dissimilar in approach to the LZW system.

It's not possible in this chapter to cover all production scenarios, as there are so many programs in use today and technical standards are changing all the time. Therefore the following discussions are limited to selected processes; if your particular need is not covered, you may at least be able to gain an understanding of general principles from those that are included.

Preparing images for print

Print images need to be saved in either TIFF (uncompressed) or EPS format for conventional press work. TIFFs are generally preferred as they are more compact than EPSs. On the other hand, EPSs perform better on some imagesetters. You can also specify whites to be transparent when 1-bit (Bitmap) images are saved in this format. Duotones can only be saved in EPS format whilst images with clipping paths usually need to be saved as EPSs to be accepted by host programs.

Colour images then need converting from RGB to CMYK. The conversion process takes into account the colour profile of the target printing press.

Furthermore all continuous tone images, colour and greyscale, need tonal adjustment to compensate for inevitable dot gain: their input settings need to compensate for the darkening of midtones; their output settings for the filling-in of shadow areas.

Finally Unsharp Mask needs to be applied to compensate for the softening of edges in the halftoning process.

✚ QuarkXPress is one program which requires images with clipping paths to be saved in EPS format.

All images

Saving a copy of your document in TIFF format

① Make a copy of the image by using the Save As procedure and save it in a different folder. Choose the TIFF format.

The TIFF Options dialog box will be displayed (see Figure 15.1).

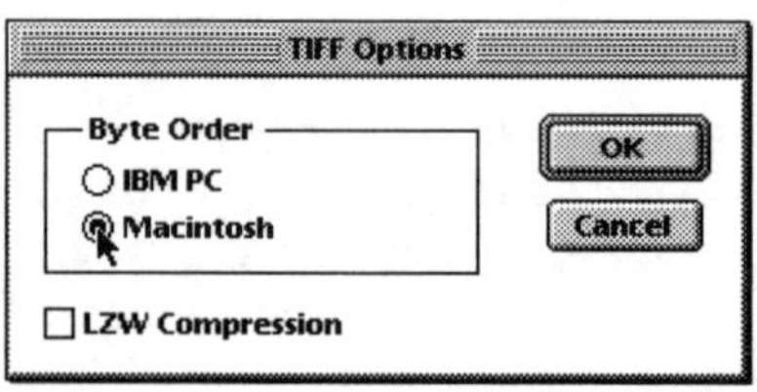

Figure 15.1 The Tiff Options dialog box

② Click IBM PC or Macintosh and uncheck LZW Compression.

③ Click OK.

Saving a copy of your document in EPS format

① Make a copy of the image by using the Save As procedure and save it in a different folder. Choose the EPS format.

The EPS Format dialog box will be displayed (see Figure 15.2).

② Choose IBM PC or Macintosh (8-bits/pixels) from the Preview pop-up menu.

③ Choose Off (single file) from the DCS pop-up menu and ASCII or Binary in the Encoding pop-up menu.

④ Choose a path from the Path pop-up menu, if you wish a clipping path to be included.

⑤ Uncheck Include Halftone Screens and Transfer Functions.

⑥ Click OK.

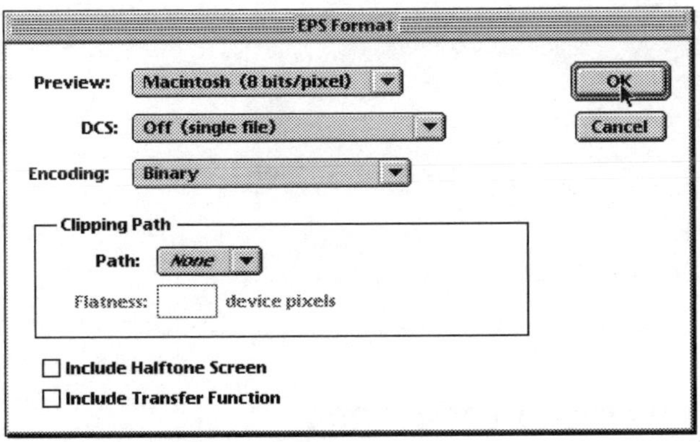

Figure 15.2 The EPS Format dialog box

Colour images only

Converting from RGB to CMYK

① Choose Colour Settings… from the Edit menu. The Colour Settings dialog box will be displayed (see Figure 15.3).

② Choose a pre-press option from the Settings pop-up menu.

③ Under Working Spaces, choose a coated, uncoated or newsprint option from the CMYK pop-up menu. If the paper stock you plan to use is matt or gloss coated choose Coated. If you plan to use an uncoated stock, such as a cartridge or stationery paper, choose Uncoated.

④ Click OK.

⑤ Choose CMYK from the Mode sub-menu in the Image menu to make the conversion.

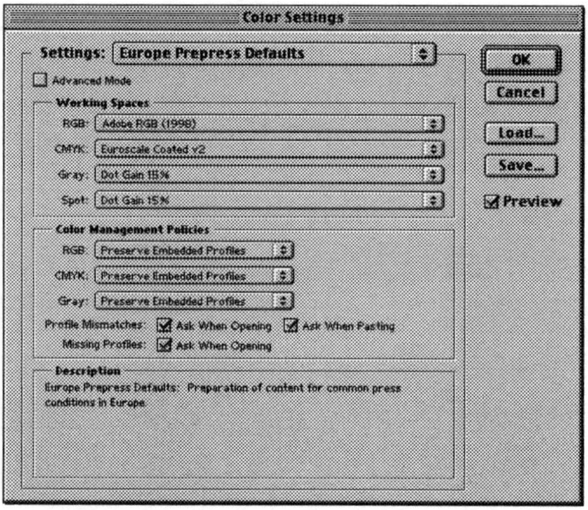

Figure 15.3 The Colour Settings dialog box

Greyscale and colour images only

The brightness levels of greyscale and CMYK images when output are affected by gamma settings in the Colour Settings dialog box. These settings compensate for dot gain on press; they alter the brightness levels of images, rather than their on-screen representation.

If images print too dark with these settings, you can make adjustments to both types of image using the Levels control.

Compensating for dot gain

① Choose Levels… from the Adjust sub-menu in the Image menu. The Levels dialog box will be displayed.

② Move the left Output slider to the right to 'open up' the blacks. This adjustment effectively lightens all tones in the image, including the very dark tones, so that they don't end up as black areas without tonal differentiation. Your printer will advise you on the appropriate setting after examining a colour proof.

③ Either:

Move the central Input slider to the left to further lighten the image.

Or:

Enter a value of between 1.25 and 1.75 in the central Input Levels field. Your printer will advise you on the appropriate setting after examining a colour proof.

④ Click OK.

Sharpening images

Apply Unsharp Mask as described in Chapter 9.

Preparing images for composite printing

Images for composite or digital printing often need to remain in RGB and saved as uncompressed TIFFs.

The colour profile for your printer should be chosen from the RGB pop-up menu under Working Spaces in the ColorSync Workflow. This work-flow is one of eight listed in the Colour Settings dialog box. If your particular printer is absent from the list, copy its profile into the ColourSync folder. Once you have done this return to the Colour Settings dialog box where it should then be listed.

Proofing images from Photoshop

The following covers some of the controls used for proofing documents on a composite printer.

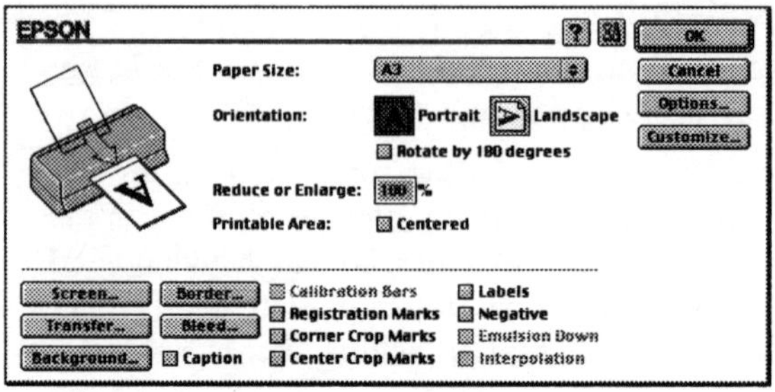

Figure 15.4 An example of Page Setup controls

Checking the Page Setup

① Choose Page Setup… from the File menu. The Page Set-up dialog box will be displayed (see Figure 15.4).

② Choose the paper size to be printed on.

③ Select the image orientation to suit the document.

④ Check Calibration bars, if a progressive greyscale bar (or progressive colour bar in the case of CMYK) is required.

⑤ Check Registration Marks, if required.

⑥ Check Corner Crop Marks, if required.

⑦ Click Screen…. Check Use Printer's Default Screens.

⑧ Click OK and then Click OK.

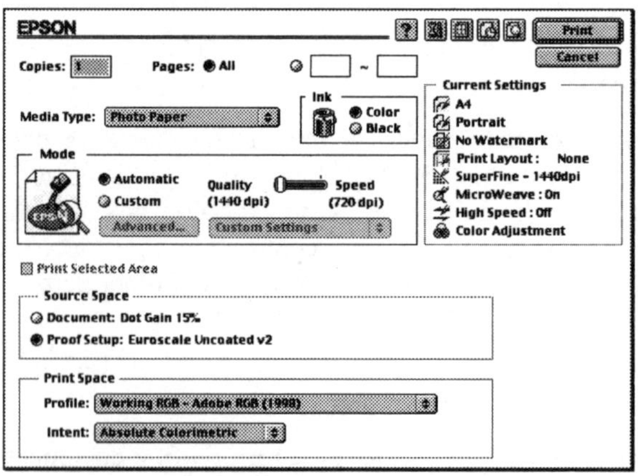

Figure 15.5 An example of Print controls

Printing the image

① Choose Print... from the File menu. The printer's dialog box will be displayed (see Figure 15.5).

② Enter the number of copies required within Copies.

③ Under Encoding, check Binary.

④ Click Print.

Preparing images for screen

Colour images should remain in RGB for on-screen delivery but their bit-depth usually needs to be reduced from 24-bit to 16- or 8-bit or less.

16-bit colour images display 65 536 colours, giving you museum quality – 'so-called photo-realism' – so there's invariably no need to maintain images at any bit depth higher than this.

8-bit images can display up to 256 colours and because their colour range can be drawn from any one of the 16.7 million or so colours, colour quality can be exceptional.

Greyscale and Bitmap images can remain as they are unless they need to be indexed, in which case they need to be converted to RGB mode.

Whether indexed or not, images must be saved in appropriate file formats. Web images are usually saved in GIF, JPEG or PNG format, all of which are hardware-independent. Images for multimedia projects are mostly saved in PICT format.

✚ Indexing is a system which refers files to a colour table for their colour range. The number of colours a file refers to depends on its bit-depth. The colour table can include any of the 16.7 million or so colours capable of being displayed, or be restricted to a sub-set of these colours.

Optimizing images for the web

When optimizing images, image quality is balanced against download times.

Graphic subjects, such as logos, should be saved as GIFs or 8-bit PNGs whereas photographs should be saved as JPEGs or 24-bit PNGs. The 8-bit formats work best with images containing areas of flat colour whereas the 24-bit formats work best with images containing lots of pixel variation.

As regards download times, JPEGs surprisingly generally take a shorter time than GIFs. PNGs, in both 8- and 24-bit form, tend to take the longest, but much depends on image content for all four types.

Whilst all the formats described offer interlacing, only GIF and PNG support transparency. GIF and 8-bit PNG have 1-bit transparency masks – image areas are either fully opaque or fully transparent – but you can matt in a background colour to give the appearance of variable transparency if you so wish. 24-bit PNGs have 8-bit transparency masks as standard so matting is not required.

Optimizing images

This process can be applied to unsliced or sliced images.

① Open an RGB image.

② Choose Save for Web… from the File menu. The Save for Web dialog box will be displayed (see Figure 15.6).

③ Click the 2-up or the 4-up tabs. 2-up displays the original image with one preview image. 4-up displays the original image with three preview images.

④ Click within a preview image. For sliced images, select a slice using the Slice Select tool.

⑤ Choose an option from the Settings pop-up menu. These options represent starter settings.

⑥ Choose options from the pop-up menus to further optimize the image (see next section).

⑦ Check, if available, Interlaced (Progressive), Transparent or ICC Profile as required. The preview will be optimized to the new settings. Beneath the preview, the file format, file size and download time is listed.

⑧ Select and optimize further slices (sliced images only).

⑨ Repeat steps 4–8 for other previews if you wish to compare different optimizations.

⑩ Click within the preferred preview.

⑪ Click OK. The Save Optimized As dialog box will be displayed.

⑫ Name the file, locate and open folder in which to save the file.

⑬ Click Save.

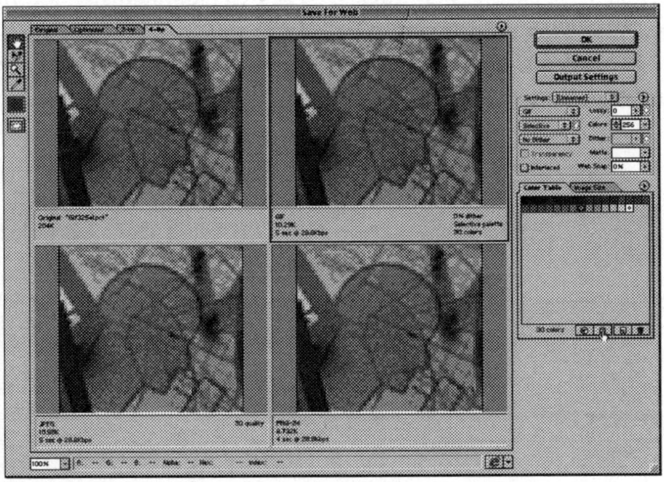

Figure 15.6 Save for Web dialog box

! In ImageReady the Optimize palette replaces the Save for Web dialog box. Before you save the file, click Output Settings to specify whether you wish to create an HTML file with or without linked images, or just save the images themselves.

Optimize settings

Optimized file format

The chosen file format. Its level of compression is controlled in either the Lossy field (in the case of GIFs) or the Compression Quality pop-menu (in the case of JPEGs).

Blur

Choose to blur an image to reduce JPEG artifacts, the tiled effect which disfigures heavily compressed images.

Colour reduction algorithms

Choose Selective (Selective combines a mix of Perceptual and Adaptive) or choose Web and set the number of colours in the Colours field.

The Perceptual palette includes image colours which are more important from a perceptual point of view. The Adaptive palette weights colours according to their frequency in an image. Selective combines the best of both palettes. The Web palette moves colours to the nearest web colour. This palette is limited to 216 colours but it has the theoretical advantage of displaying colours consistently in all browser situations.

Colour

Follow the procedure in the next section.

Web Snap

Enter a figure above zero if you wish colours that are close to web colours to snap to the web palette. The higher the figure the more likely it is that colours will snap.

Dithering algorithm

Choose None if banding does not occur in tonal areas. Otherwise choose Dither. Set the amount of dither in the Dither field.

Transparency

Enable Transparency if you wish to retain image transparency. The image must be on a layer and have transparent areas for this to work.

Matte

If Transparency is enabled, define a colour to blend with transparent pixels. This colour should be chosen to match the background colour of the web page.

Interlacing/progressive

Enable either if you wish the image to be downloaded in multiple passes.

ICC Profile

Choose to include ICC profile in JPEGs based on Photoshop's colour compensation.

Reducing the number of colours

① Choose the maximum number of colours in the Colours field. The colours will be displayed in the Colour Table. Amongst these colours may be ones you don't wish to drop when you reduce the number of colours.

② Select the Eyedropper tool in the dialog box and click a colour in the image you wish to keep. It will be outlined in the Colour Table.

③ Select the outlined colour in the Colour Table and click the Lock icon.

④ Repeat the process for other key colours.

⑤ Then reduce the number of colours in the Colours field until the lowest acceptable image quality is reached.

⑥ Click OK.

! In ImageReady the Optimize and Colour Table palettes replace the Save for Web dialog box.

Saving web pages and web features

Web pages, complete with rollover effects, imagemaps and animations, are first optimized and then saved along with an HTML document containing links and Javascript.

Optimizing is usually achieved in ImageReady, with optimized documents saved using the Save Optimized command (see Chapter 2). Small-scale documents can alternatively be optimized as part of Photoshop's Save for Web process (described earlier in this chapter).

Preparing images for multimedia projects

Although a variety of file formats can be accepted by multimedia programs, in practice the PICT format is most widely used. Macromedia Director, QuarkImmedia, VideoFusion and Adobe Premiere all support this format.

Images can be 1-bit, 2-bit, 4-bit, 8-bit, 16-bit or 32-bit, depending on the authoring or editing program, image subject and colour strategy you adopt.

If you are partly targeting older computers with limited colour support, images may need to be indexed to 8-bit or less.

Some programs help to further reduce file sizes by automatically compressing imported images. Others enable you to reduce their bit-depth once imported.

Indexing an image

① Open an RGB image.

② Choose Indexed... from the Mode sub-menu in the Image menu. The Indexed Colour dialog box will be displayed (see Figure 15.7).

③ Choose Exact from the Palette pop-up menu if you wish to use the actual colours in the image. This option is only available for images with 256 colours or less.

Or: Choose System (Macintosh) or System (Windows) from the Palette pop-up menu if you wish to use the standard Macintosh or Windows colours.

Or: Choose Local (Selective) from the Palette pop-up menu if you wish to maintain photo-realistic colour levels.

④ Enter a lower figure than 256 in the Colours field if you wish to further reduce the number of colours in an image. Otherwise leave at 256.

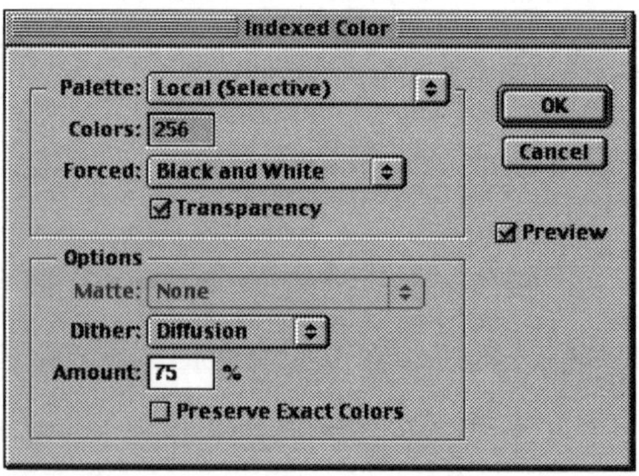

Figure 15.7 The Indexed Colour dialog box

⑤ Experiment with either None or Diffusion from the Dither pop-up menu.

⑥ Click OK.

! In Photoshop 3.0 choose Indexed Colour... in the Mode menu to display this dialog box.

Saving the file as a PICT

① Save the image choosing the PICT format. The PICT File Options dialog box will be displayed (see Figure 15.8).

② Select a Resolution and Compression option, as required.

③ Click OK.

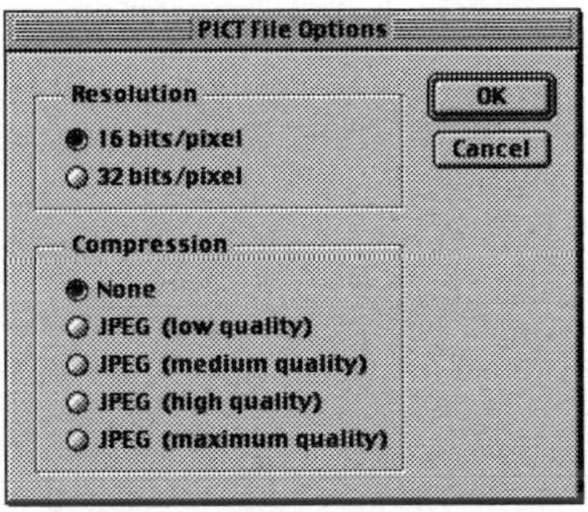

Figure 15.8 The PICT File Options dialog box

Working with indexed images

Since only one set of 256 colours is available at any one time on 8-bit monitors, indexing needs to be planned with care if unpleasant colour shifts are to be avoided.

The complication of displaying images together or in sequence with different custom palettes may outweigh the advantage gained in colour fidelity.

The problem can be removed completely by restricting yourself to the system palette or imposing a single common custom palette throughout a project, covering both content and interface elements.

Alternatively, any number of common palettes can be used within a project, as appropriate.

A common palette can be developed and applied within Photoshop, within an authoring program such as Macromedia Director or using Equilibrium's graphics translator DeBabelizer.

Creating a common palette within Photoshop

① Create a large new blank document.

② Paste the images into the blank document.

③ Index the combined image using the Adaptive palette with any dither option selected. Click OK.

④ Choose Colour Table... from the Mode sub-menu in the Image menu. The Colour Table dialog box will be displayed.

⑤ Click Save to save the colour table.

⑥ Close the combined image.

⑦ Open one of the original images.

⑧ Choose Indexed Colour... from the Mode sub-menu in the Image menu. The Indexed Colour dialog box will be displayed.

⑨ Click Custom... with no dither. Click OK. The Custom dialog box will be displayed.

⑩ Click Load. A directory dialog box will be displayed.

⑪ Use the directory dialog box controls to locate the saved colour table.

⑫ Click Open. Click OK to apply the palette. The image will be indexed using the colour table.

⑬ Repeat steps 6 to 11 for the other images.

Preparing images for colour slides

Images can be output as colour slides using a slide film recorder, a device comprising a black-and-white cathode-ray tube attached to a 35 mm or large-format camera.

Images need to be in 24-bit, RGB mode and without an embedded profile for this type of output and especially adjusted to cater for the difference in gamma between monitors and photographic film.

A variety of file formats can be used, including Photoshop 3.0, PICT and TIFF (either compressed or uncompressed).

Film recorders measure resolution in terms of image size, such as 4K (4096×2732 pixels). Think of a recorder as having a number of grids, one for each outputting resolution (2K, 4K, 8K, etc.). To get the best output from a recorder, the image must be equal to or slightly smaller than the dimensions of a grid (in pixels). Otherwise the image will have to be resized. A resolution of 4K, incidently, exceeds the resolution of Ektachrome so a higher resolution adds to processing time without increasing image sharpness.

The optimum image size for 5×4 transparencies is 4096×2732 pixels, giving an approximate file size of 35 MB and a resolution of 4K. Any ppi resolution will do, as the slide production house will change it to suit their requirements. The optimum image size for 35 mm transparencies is 2048 ×1366 pixels, giving an approximate file size of 10 MB and a resolution of 2K. As for 5×4 transparencies, any ppi resolution will do.

Setting gamma levels for slides

① Choose Levels... from the Adjust sub-menu in the Image menu. The Levels dialog box will be displayed.

② Enter 2.2 in the central Input Levels field.

③ Click OK.

Summary

Images need to be in the correct mode and file format for a given use.

Colour images usually need to be converted to CMYK and their output and/or gamma settings adjusted prior to going to press.

Whilst web images tend to be optimized in Save for Web control multimedia images are indexed using the Indexed Colour command.

Images for film output need their gamma settings adjusted.

16 ALLOCATING MEMORY

Photoshop is memory-hungry: it needs adequate memory to process large files and to perform complex tasks with sufficient speed and efficiency. This memory is provided by RAM, your system's built-in memory, combined with scratch disk space (free space on a designated hard disk).

Its scratch disk system is always on and normally works best when your computer's own virtual memory system is switched on. Provided that you have sufficient contiguous scratch disk space on the Macintosh, you can allocate to Photoshop an amount that is slightly less than the largest unused block in RAM (taking into account the preferred size of your scanning program and any other programs you wish to run at the same time as Photoshop). On PCs, you can allocate to Photoshop a percentage of the available RAM instead.

So if you wish to get the best performance out of Photoshop you will need to address three memory aspects.

- The system's virtual memory (Macintosh only)
- Photoshop's scratch disk system
- Photoshop's memory allocation

! Note that all the above points also apply to ImageReady.

Switching on the Macintosh's virtual memory

① Choose Control Panels from the Apple menu. Double-click on the Memory icon. The Memory control panel will be displayed (see Figure 16.1).

② Click On under Virtual memory.

③ Set the amount to 1 MB more than the available built-in memory.

④ Click the On radio button under Modern Memory Manager or 32-bit addressing.

⑤ Reduce the amount in the Cache Size field to the minimum (this is optional).

⑥ Close the control panel.

⑦ Restart your computer.

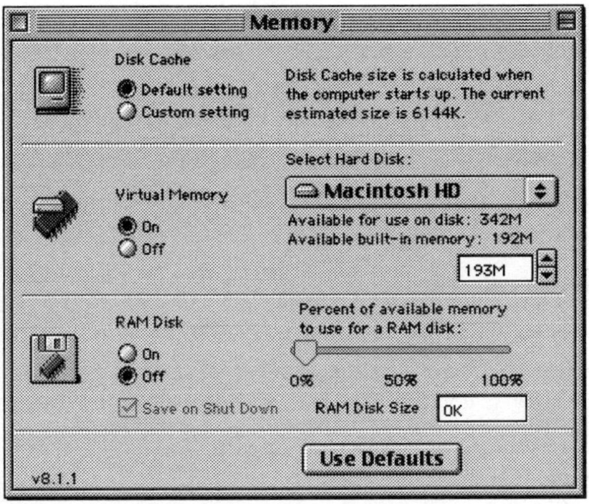

Figure 16.1 The Memory control panel on the Macintosh

Ascertaining free disk (Macintosh)

Photoshop 6.0 requires a minimum of 64 MB of free disk space.

① Double-click the disk icon (chosen as a scratch disk) on the Desktop.

② The amount available in MB will be shown below the title bar of the window (see Figure 16.2).

③ Repeat steps 1 and 2 for any secondary disk and add both totals together.

Figure 16.2 Available disk capacity information below the title bar

Ascertaining free disk (Windows)

Photoshop 6.0 requires a minimum of 64 MB of free disk space.

① Double-click the disk icon (chosen as a scratch disk) on the Desktop.

② The amount available in MB will be shown on the title bar of the window.

③ Repeat steps 1 and 2 for any secondary disk and add both totals together.

Photoshop's memory allocation

You can now allocate the amount of memory you wish Photoshop to use. Photoshop 6.0 requires a minimum of 32 MB of application RAM (64 MB recommended).

Altering the memory allocation (Macintosh)

① Choose Quit from the File menu, if Photoshop is loaded.

② Choose Finder from the Applications menu on the far right of the menu bar.

③ Locate the Photoshop program icon (see Figure 16.3). If it is greyed return to step 1.

④ Select (click once) the Photoshop program icon.

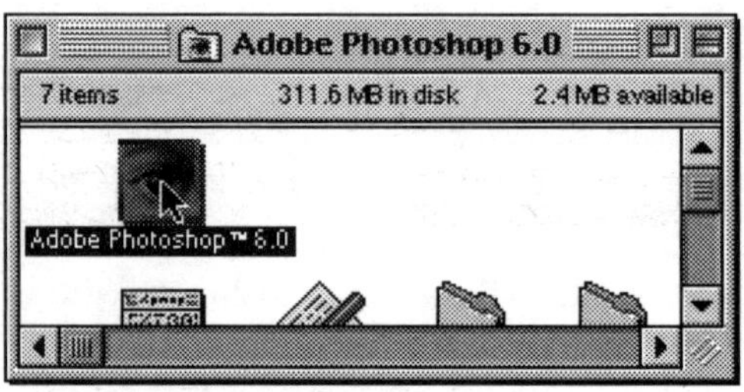

Figure 16.3 The Photoshop program icon

⑤ Choose Get Info… from the Finder's File menu. The Adobe Photoshop 6.0 Info dialog box will be displayed (see Figure 16.4).

⑥ Enter an amount in the Preferred size field.

⑦ Close the dialog box.

⑧ Re-load Photoshop in the usual way. The system software will set aside the memory you allocated.

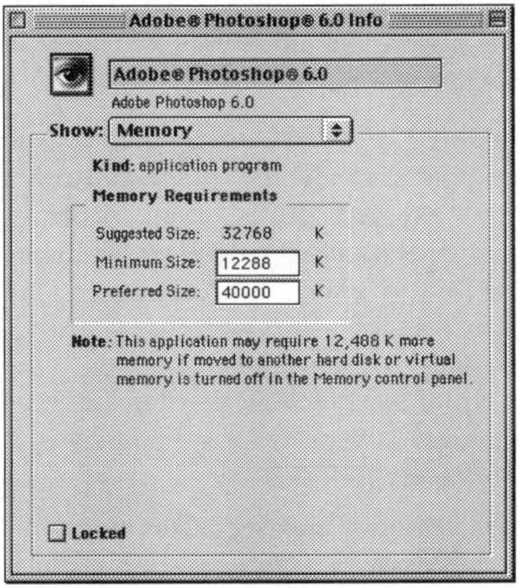

Figure 16.4 Photoshop's Info dialog box

! The amount you enter in the Preferred size field must be smaller than the amount of free disk space on your chosen scratch disk(s). See *Ascertaining free disk space*, page 185.

Calculate the preferred size as follows: take the Available built-in memory figure (from the About this Macintosh dialog box or the Memory control panel), e.g. 25 000K, subtract the System Software figure (from the About this Macintosh dialog box), e.g. 5000K, and the Preferred size of your scanner program (from its Info box), e.g. 5000K. Multiply the figure left by 90%. (25 000 – 5 000 – 5 000 = 15 000. 15 000×90% = 13 500.)

Altering the memory allocation (Windows)

① Choose Memory and Cache Size… from the Preferences sub-menu in the Photoshop's Edit menu. The Memory and Cache Size set of preferences will be displayed.

② Enter an amount in the Memory field of no more than, say, 70%.

③ Click OK.

④ Quit and re-load Photoshop in the usual way. The system software will set aside the memory you allocated.

Photoshop's scratch disks

Photoshop's scratch disk system is always on and is used whenever it's unable to hold a complete image on the computer's RAM.

It 'shunts' data that the RAM can't hold onto disks which you designate for this purpose; these can include your start-up disk (which normally is your internal hard disk) or any external drives, even ejectables. Remember any disk drives you target need to have sufficient contiguous space to act as an efficient medium for this work.

Choosing a scratch disk

① Choose Scratch disks… from the Preferences sub-menu in the Edit menu. The Plug-ins & Scratch Disk Preferences will be displayed (see Figure 16.5).

② Choose an option from the Primary and Secondary pop-up menus.

③ Click OK.

④ Choose Quit from the File menu and then reload Photoshop in the usual way.

! Ensure that you have at least as much scratch disk space as RAM allocated to Photoshop. Otherwise you may get a Scratch Disk Full message.

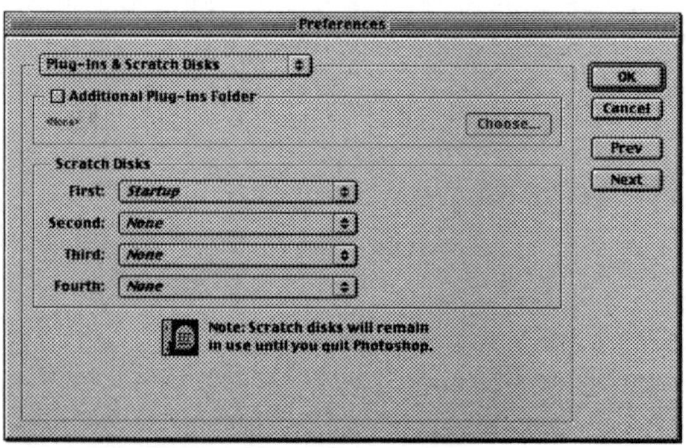

Figure 16.5 The Scratch Disk Preferences

Monitoring memory and scratch disk usage

Monitoring memory usage (Macintosh)

You can monitor memory usage when Photoshop is running.

① Choose Finder from the Applications menu on the far right of the menu bar.

② Choose About this Macintosh… from the Apple menu. The About this Macintosh dialog box will be displayed.

The Total (Built in) Memory is measured in K and beneath are listed all the loaded programs and their current memory allocations.

③ Close the dialog box.

Monitoring scratch disk usage

The scratch size information is shown in a panel at the bottom left-hand corner of the document window.

- Choose Scratch Sizes from the pop-up menu at the bottom left of the document window (see Figure 16.6). The first figure indicates how much space Photoshop is currently using. The second figure indicates the total amount of RAM available. If the first figure exceeds the second figure, Photoshop is using the scratch disk(s).

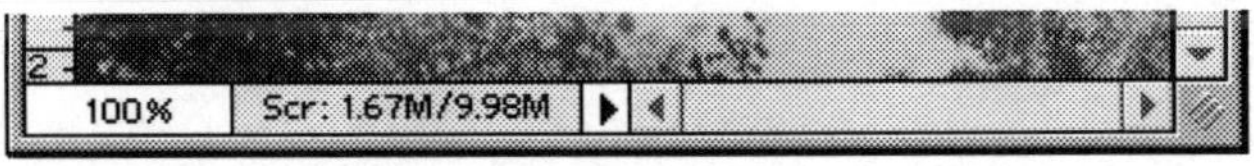

Figure 16.6 The Scratch Sizes pop-up menu

Appendix I
KEYSTROKES

Keyboard shortcuts

Painting and filling

Tool or key	*Result*
Eyedropper+Alt+click	Selects background colour
⌘+Delete	Fills with background colour
Alt+Delete	Fills with foreground colour
Shift+Delete	Displays Fill dialog box
Any painting tool+Alt	Temporarily switches to Eyedropper tool
Any paint/edit tool 1 to 9	Sets opacity, pressure or exposure for painting mode
[or]	Sets the brush size larger or smaller
Shift+[or]	Softens or hardens the brushes
Caps Lock	Changes cursor to cross-hair pointer
⌘+click	Removes colour from Swatches palette
Alt Shift+click	Adds colour to Swatches palette
Shift+click	Replaces colour in Swatches palette

Selecting and moving

Tool or key	*Result*
Shift+drag	Constrains marquee to square or circle
Alt+drag	Draws marquee from centre
Shift+Alt+drag	Adds to or subtracts from selection

Alt Shift + drag	Connects parts of separate selections
⌘	Temporarily switches to Move tool (all tools, except Pen or Grabber Hand)
⌘ + Alt +drag	Moves a copy of selection
← → ↓ ↑	Moves selection in increments of 1 pixel
⌘ + Return	Makes a selection from a path
Crop border + Esc	Cancels crop
Transform border + Esc	Cancels transform

Viewing

Tool or key	*Result*
⌘ + H	Hides all non-printing elements
Space	Grabber tool
Double-click Grabber hand	Fits image to full size window
Double-click Zoom tool	Switches to 100% magnification
Zoom tool +drag	Enlarges selected area
⌘ + += +drag	Zooms in
⌘ + −- +click	Zooms out
⌘ + Space +drag	Enlarges selected area
⌘ + Alt Space +click	Reduces image

Path editing

Tool or key	*Result*
Any pen tool + ⌘	Temporarily switches to Direct Selection tool

Editing

Tool or key	*Result*
Double-click, triple-click, quadruple-click or quintuple-click	Selects word, line, paragraph or story
⌘ Shift + <, or <,	Increases/decreases typesize by 2 pt
⌘ Alt Shift + <, / <,	Increases/decreases typesize by 10 pt
Alt + ↑ / ↓	Increases/decreases leading by 2 pt
⌘ Alt + ↑ / ↓	Increases/decreases leading by 10 pt
Shift Alt + ↑ / ↓	Increases/decreases baseline shift by 2 pt
⌘ Shift Alt + ↑ / ↓	Increases/decreases baseline shift by 10 pt

Other shortcuts

Tool or key	*Result*
⌘ + F	Applies last filter
⌘ Alt + F	Opens last filter dialog box
Control + >.	Cancels operation

Appendix II
GLOSSARY

alert box dialog box on a screen alerting you to all the consequences of a decision you are about to take

anchor point the location on a path which determines the shape and direction of the path segments extending from that location

anti Alias addition of pixels with intermediate values at the boundaries of edges to reduce the 'staircasing' effect of a bitmapped representation

ASCII short for American Standard Code for Information Interchange. Standard format for representing digital information in 8-bit chunks

baseline imaginary horizontal line on which upper and lower case letters sit; descenders extend below this line

Bézier curve method of creating shapes based on mathematical methods pioneered by Pierre Bézier

binary the base-2 numbering system that most computers use

bit smallest possible unit of information; short for binary digit

bit depth a measure of the amount of information recorded or displayed for each pixel

bitmap image made up of pixels (or dots)

brightness amount of white or black in a colour

bromide photographic paper used by imagesetters for artwork-quality prints

bureau company specializing in printing and/or imagesetting DTP documents: in this book, bureau refers also to a repro department at a printing works and a colour copy shop

cast overall colour bias

CCD short for Charge-Coupled Device: a light-sensitive chip-mounted device used in scanners to convert light into an electrical charge

character generic name for a letter, number, symbol or 'invisible'

check box small box that works as a toggle for selecting an option. When you click on an empty box, an X appears, turning it on; when you click again, the X disappears and the option is turned off

Chooser Macintosh desk accessory used to log into devices, such as printers and other computers linked to a network. Also used to enable and disable AppleTalk, Apple's native networking protocol

clipboard area of a computer's memory that holds what you last cut or copied. Paste inserts a copy of the current contents of the clipboard

clipping path a vectored path which masks areas of an image when printed

closed path a path consisting of three or more points whose first and last points are the same

CLUT short for Colour Look-Up Table: a colour indexing system used by computers to reference colours if their systems don't support the correct bit-depth to represent all colours

CMYK short for for Cyan, Magenta, Yellow and Key (black): the colour model used in the graphic arts and printing fields

contrast the relationship between the lightest and darkest areas in an image

cut-out non-rectangular image

crop marks lines which indicate the trimmed edge of pages

cursor pointer or other icon indicating the screen position of the mouse

document size in Photoshop, the overall amount of data in an image

dialog box box on a screen requesting information, or a decision, from you

direction line Bézier handle controlling the shape of curves

dpi dots per inch: measurement of the density of information in an image. Also the measurement of the resolution of printers and imagesetters. See ppi

dtp desktop publishing

drive floppy, removable or hard disk

em measure equal to the width of the square of a font size, e.g. a 15 pt em is 15 pt; corresponds roughly to the width of a capital M; used as a horizontal unit of measure – see en

en measure equal to half the width of the square of a font size, e.g. a 15 pt en is 7.5 pt; corresponds roughly to the width of a lower-case n; used as a horizontal unit of measure – see em

field in Photoshop, an area in a dialog box or palette in which you enter values
film photographic film used by imagesetters for colour separations
floating selection a moved or pasted selection which hasn't yet been blended with underlying pixels
font single character – letter, number, punctuation mark or symbol – within a type family. Often used interchangeably with the word 'typeface'
format way of saving files and transferring data

gamma measure of how compressed or expanded dark or light tones become in an image
gamut range of colours available in a particular colour system space (or mode)
GIF short for Graphic Interchange Format: most widely supported file format for web pages
greyscale depiction of grey tones between black and white: usually composed of 256 greys

halftone pattern (or screen) of dots of different sizes used to simulate a continuous tone photograph, either in colour or monochrome. Measured in lines per inch (lpi)
hue in the HSB colour space, the colour component of colour, such as red or green

I-beam cursor's shape when dealing with text
image graphic, photograph or illustration
imagemap bitmap image, with associated map file and program, containing multiple URL links
imagesetter digital phototypesetting machine capable of producing graphic images as well as type on bromide or film. Most imagesetters are PostScript-compatible
indexed colour a colour system which uses information from a file or from software as a pointer to a table of colours rather than specifying a colour directly
insertion point blinking vertical line indicating where the next keystroke will add or delete text
interpolation estimation of values between two known values. Assignment of an intermediate colour to pixel based on the colour of the surrounding pixels

JPEG short for Joint Photographic Experts Group: pronounced 'Jaypeg'. A set of standards developed for compressing and decompressing digitized images

kerning in Illustrator, inter-character spacing adjusted locally; used for styling, and optical reasons
keystrokes use of modifier keys with other keys to execute a command
keypad the numeric keys on the right of the keyboard (extended version)

layer transparent plane that helps organize images and controls how they stack upon each other in a composite image
leading repeat distance between lines of text, usually measured between baselines. Pronounced 'ledding'
lpi short for lines per inch: the measurement of a halftone screen
LZW Lempel, Ziv and Welsh: a lossless compression algorithm

menu list of commands
modifier keys keys which modify the effect of a character key when pressed. The standard modifier keys are [⌘], [Alt], [Shift], [Control] and [Caps Lock]
monochrome tonal original, in shades of only one colour, such as black

original artwork or photographs used as a subject for scanning

Pantone Matching System shortened to PMS: proprietory colour matching system used in the graphic arts and printing industries
path line element comprising one or more segments
photo litho short for photo lithography: the primary technology for printing books, magazines and brochures
PICT Apple's native file format
pixel short for picture element: the smallest distinct unit of a bitmapped image
Plug-in program which extends the functionality of Photoshop
PNG short for Portable Network Graphics: colour file format for web pages using lossless compression algorithms
point (of path) – see anchor point
point unit of measure; measuring close to 1/72 inch and very roughly one-third of a millimetre
PostScript device-independent page description language developed by Adobe and used by most DTP programs

ppi short for pixels per inch: measurement of the density of information in an image. See dpi

process colours the CMYK colours used to reproduce colour photographs and illustrations

profile description of the imaging performance of a computer device; used for colour management purposes

program sequence of instructions that tells a computer what to do: also called software

printer digital desktop or commercial device for printing or proofing documents mostly using laser, ink jet, die sublimation or thermal wax technologies

QuickDraw programming routines that enable the Macintosh to display graphic elements on screen and to output text and images to certain QuickDraw printers

radio buttons group of small buttons for selecting a option, only one of which can be on at one time

raster image bitmap image

rasterize to convert vector graphics into bitmap images

RAM memory a computer uses to store information it's processing at any given moment

registration marks marks included on film separations for the purposes of colour registration

remapping reforming the pixels of a bitmap image

resampling adding, deleting or re-arranging pixels within a bitmapped image

resolution the density of data in a digital image, measured in pixels per linear inch (ppi)

retouch removal of defects, dust. scratches, etc. within an image

RGB the colour model used by monitors and within multimedia projects, based on red, green and blue

saturation in the HSB colour space, a measure of the amount of grey in a colour. The higher the grey content, the lower the saturation

scan bitmap image; image digitized by a scanner

scratch disk designated disk used by Photoshop to temporarily off-load data it can't hold on RAM

TIFF short for Tagged Image File Format, a popular file format for saving bitmap images
tracking word and letter spacing adjusted locally; used for copyfitting, styling and to improve readability
transform to move, rotate, scale, shear or reflect an image
trim marks lines printed outside the edge of a document page for aligning guillotines
TWAIN generic driver used to access scanning controls from within Photoshop
typeface collection of letters, numbers, punctuation marks and symbols with an identifiable and consistent appearance. Often used interchangeably with the word 'font'

vector the numerical location of a point in terms of x and y coordinates
vector graphic drawing or object defined mathematically; sometimes called object oriented
virtual memory a means of using storage memory on a disk to supplement RAM
vignette soft edge given to images

Keys

Alt key: modifier key used in conjunction with other keys, often providing an alternative function

Back Space/Delete key: used to delete selections and, within the Type dialog box, to delete text to the left of the insertion point

Caps Lock key: used to turn tool icons into a cross-hair

Command key (with an Apple on it): modifier key used with other keys to issue commands

Control key: modifier key used in connection with other keys

Enter key: used to close dialog boxes

Return key: used to separate paragraphs within the Type dialog box and close dialog boxes

Shift key: modifier key used to capitalize letters and constrain pointer movement, amongst other things

Tab key: used to hide and show palettes